LUIS
SUAREZ

Dr. Alec Patton
apatton@hightechhigh.org

LUIS SUAREZ

THE BIOGRAPHY OF THE WORLD'S
MOST CONTROVERSIAL FOOTBALLER

FRANK WORRALL

JOHN BLAKE

Published by John Blake Publishing Ltd,
3 Bramber Court, 2 Bramber Road,
London W14 9PB, England

www.johnblakepublishing.co.uk

www.facebook.com/johnblakebooks **f**
twitter.com/jbbooks **t**

This edition published in 2014

ISBN: 978 1 78418 019 5

British Library Cataloguing-in-Publication Data:

A catalogue record for this book is available from the British Library.

Design by www.envydesign.co.uk

Printed in Great Britain by CPI Group (UK) Ltd

1 3 5 7 9 10 8 6 4 2

Papers used by John Blake Publishing are natural, recyclable products made
from wood grown in sustainable forests. The manufacturing processes
conform to the environmental regulations of the country of origin.

Every attempt has been made to contact the relevant copyright-holders,
but some were unobtainable. We would be grateful if the appropriate
people could contact us.

This book is dedicated to Roy Stone, Jo Hernon,
Nathan Griffiths, Mark Bengoechea and Carole Theobald:
all great friends and loyal Liverpool FC fans.

ACKNOWLEDGEMENTS

SPECIAL THANKS: Chris Mitchell, James Hodgkinson, Anna Marx, Joanna Kennedy and all at John Blake Publishing. Alan Feltham, Ben Felsenburg at the *Daily Mail* and Alex Butler at *The Sunday Times*.

THANKS: Allie Collins, Mike Gould, Duncan Williams, Ian Rondeau, Colin Forshaw, Ash Hussein, Gary Edwards, Adrian Baker, Ben Green, Clive Martin, Steven Gordon, Lee Clayton, Darren O'Driscoll, Martin Creasy, Lee Hassall, John Fitzpatrick, Paul Hazeldine, Nigel Wareing and Tom Henderson Smith.

NOT FORGETTING: Angela, Frankie and Jude, Natalie, Barbara, Frank, Bob and Stephen, Gill, Lucy, Alex, Suzanne, Michael and William.

CONTENTS

INTRODUCTION

When I was asked to put together a biography on Luis Suarez, I said 'yes' immediately. It was a chance to dig deep and find out what motivates a world-class player. To learn about his background, his hinterland and exactly what formed and moulded him as a footballer... and a person. The weeks of research and interviews proved more than worthwhile when I finally got around to writing the book. For what I realised a couple of weeks in was this: not only was I compiling a biography on Liverpool's best player of the modern era but I was also compiling a biography on a man who is arguably THE best player of the modern era.

And, beyond that, arguably Liverpool's best player ever (along with the legendary Kenny Dalglish) and arguably the best foreign player ever to grace these shores (along with Cristiano Ronaldo) and arguably the best striker in the world right now, given that Ronaldo and Messi play more between the lines than Suarez.

So what initially had been a simple commission eventually became a privilege as it struck me that I was doing the first biog ever on a man who can conceivably stake the claims above; that I was looking between the lines at the life of the best footballer in the world right now – and the man who had won both of the Footballer of the Year awards for 2013–14.

Of course, given his nature and controversies, Luis Suarez will always polarise opinions among everyone who loves the beautiful game – fans, fellow pros, managers and even football-club chairmen. Steve Bruce, the much-travelled manager of Hull City, for example, agrees wholeheartedly with me that Luis is the best striker in the world.

As this book went to the printers in the summer of 2014, Bruce said,

Never mind Luis being the Premier League's top player. On current form, he's got to be the best in the world. There is just nobody around who you can say is better than him right now. Neither Cristiano Ronaldo nor the Barcelona trio of Andres Iniesta, Xavi and Neymar – and Lionel Messi can't come into the equation because he's been out injured so long.

OK, we've all done stupid things on the pitch and Suarez has had his moments. But he has cleaned up his act over the first half of this season.

Luis's Uruguayan co-striker Edinson Cavani agreed with Bruce that Luis was the best in the world and added that he believed England and the striker's constant critics would suffer as a result when the nations met in competitive action. Cavani said, 'Luis Suarez is very familiar with this England team and his experience in the Premier League will help us beat them. He has nothing to prove to anyone but for what the English media have inflicted, we look forward to silencing his critics. For me he is the best striker in the world right now and I'm sure he will retain his present form to the World Cup.' How right Cavani would be proved about that as Suarez returned to haunt them in June 2014 with that brilliant brace in the World Cup group stage.

And Liverpool boss Brendan Rodgers also felt the need to defend his star man when Luis came under criticism every week over alleged diving and bad sportsmanship. Rodgers was particularly aggrieved when Suarez was singled out after HE was the victim of a Robert Huth stamp in a 0–0 draw with Stoke City.

Rodgers said,

As manager of this football club, I find it incredible that in nearly all the coverage about Luis Suarez this weekend, very little focus has been placed on the fact that he was actually the victim of a stamping incident within the first five minutes of the game.

At this moment there seems to be one set of rules for Luis and another set for everyone else. Diving and simulation is obviously a wider issue in football and one that we all agree has to be eradicated from our game but there were other incidents this weekend that didn't seem to generate the same coverage. No one should be distracted by the real issue here, both at Anfield and at another game played on Sunday, when Luis and another player were hurt in off-the-ball incidents that went unpunished but were caught on TV cameras.

I believe some people need to develop a sense of perspective and I also believe in this moment the vilification of Luis is both wrong and unfair. I will continue to protect the values, spirit and people of this great club and game while searching for a consistent level of results in order to make progress on the field.

Yet on the other side of the coin, many others considered Luis's temperament held him back; that his unpredictability and tendency to fly off the handle at other players diminished him. I can understand that view when you look back at his 'Cannibal' interludes in Amsterdam and with Chelsea's Branislav Ivanovic – and, of course, that self-destructive chomp on Italy's Giorgio Chiellini in the 2014 World Cup. And his disciplinary record over the years has hardly been that of a model pro.

Oldham boss Lee Johnson called Luis 'a dirty rat' and 'horrible' before the Latics met Liverpool in an FA Cup class earlier in 2014. It was an insult but a view held by many pundits and fans who still find it hard to forgive Suarez for his indiscretions. However, even Johnson qualified his comment by making it clear that he also knew Luis to be world class and a star act.

Johnson had formed his view after turning out as a player for his former club Bristol City in a friendly against Luis when he was at Ajax Amsterdam in 2009. Johnson said, 'He's like a dirty street rat and I mean that in the best possible way. He's sharp and horrible – all that is in admiration for him because he's a winner. He has that desire to be better today than he was yesterday. I played against Suarez for Bristol City and I failed miserably – he scored. I remember asking, "Who was that lad up front?" He wasn't well known then. I was like, "Who on earth is that?" I was meant to stop the ball up to him but you just can't. Sometimes players are just too good.'

And Swansea City defender Ashley Williams went so far as to admit that he despised Luis and would like to 'knock him out'. Williams said, 'Suarez dived more than any other player I've played against before – it was so bad I was genuinely shocked. Throughout the game, he just dived down and screamed at any given moment. Suarez has that aura about him that says "I'm untouchable" and his manner and behaviour made me want to knock him out. I'd go as far as to say that the manner in which he approached the game, with utter contempt for us all, means that he's streets ahead of any player I've truly disliked since I've been in the Premier League.'

Strong stuff but criticisms Luis would rebuff in the best way possible – by giving weekly masterclasses in goal scoring and model behaviour during the 2013–14 season. In that superb campaign – as he proved week in and week out that he was simply the best player in the Premier League – Luis Suarez will be best remembered for his classy play, his incredible wealth of goals and the way he almost single-handedly propelled Liverpool to their finest season for many a year.

It is certainly true that, if you took away Luis's goals and contributions, Liverpool would not have done as well as they have. They are not a one-man team – what with Gerrard, Sturridge and Coutinho – but they would also not be the same team if they lost the services of Suarez. He is a genius and deserved every accolade that came his way over the last season.

Koppites had admitted they would be devastated if Liverpool lost him but they knew one thing for sure: his mooted departure to Barcelona would cost the Catalan giants far in advance of the desultory £40.1 million Arsenal offered for him in the summer of 2013. No, if Gareth Bale set Real Madrid back €100 million (around £86 million), Luis is worth £100 million in sterling, let alone euros.

Don't get me wrong, Bale is good, very good. But he is not in the same league as Suarez in terms of goals and importance to a team. Take Bale out of Madrid's starting eleven, and they will still win most games. But put Luis in Madrid's starting eleven instead of Bale and the results would, I believe, be even better.

When you buy Luis Suarez, you buy the guarantee of goals galore. He is a one-man goal machine who has scored in abundance from youth teams through to Liverpool.

And when you understand his background, you do start to understand the man.

Suarez was one of seven siblings, brought up in relative poverty in Uruguay for many years by his mother after his father walked out on the family. His life has been punctuated by abandonment and emotional distress: whenever he seemed to find happiness, it was rudely snatched away from him. He was the little boy left crying in the corner... alone and sad. At six years old, his parents told him they were leaving his beloved hometown and pals in El Salto for the big city of Montevideo. His unhappiness was such that he would return home in the school summer holidays and stay with his grandmother. His father abandoned him and he finally found happiness with his sweetheart Sofia in Montevideo – only for her to also leave for Europe and Barcelona. He was the undisputed star of the Nacional youth team in Montevideo but was threatened with the boot there.

It seemed throughout his life that he would take one step forward only to then suffer two steps back.

It was only at Liverpool that he finally felt secure after a lifetime of anxiety – and it is to the eternal credit of Kop boss Brendan Rodgers that is the case. He stood by his man when many were calling for him to be sold. And, eventually, the penny dropped with Luis: he realised that Rodgers had stuck his neck out for him and started to repay him. He repaid loyalty with loyalty and his goals set Liverpool up for a superb season in the Premier League.

At the end of the campaign, Luis declared himself happy with his life and his lot on Merseyside. It appeared the wanderer had finally come home – only for him to self-destruct in the World Cup and leave Liverpool FC with the unenviable choice of keeping him and his goals, or letting him leave for Barcelona and losing the man who had led them back to the promised land of the Champions League.

Brendan Rodgers would admit it was the hardest decision of his footballing career – one that could define his and Liverpool's future. This is the warts and all story of Luis Suarez – the most controversial footballer in the world today. A troubled genius who could beat another team on his own with his full array of dazzling skills, yet a man who could never gain the upper hand when it came to his own self-destructive inner demons. Truly, a Diego Maradona of the modern footballing era.

Frank Worrall
July 2014

CHAPTER ONE

STREET FIGHTER

Suarez's father would always shrug his shoulders and say, 'Well, he was born to be a footballer,' as little Luis carried on kicking a ball out onto the cobbled streets with his mates when friends came to visit. Rodolfo would eventually have to rush from the cramped house the family of nine shared in El Salto and forcibly bring his son home to say a swift 'hello' to their visitors before they headed off home. Long after they had gone, little Luis would continue to play in the dark, trying to win every match as the kids of the neighbourhood used bin lids for goalposts and ducked in and out as cars travelled up and down the road.

Every goal was the winner in the cup final – or in the World Cup – and was greeted with squeals of delight. Every goal lifted their spirits and encouraged them to dream. Luis might only have been four but, like all his playing pals, he was driven by a desire to make the big-time; often their games in the street would end in punches, such was the determination in their play.

They may have been young but they were determined to win. It wasn't unusual for Luis to scoop up his football and run for home with it under his arm if he was on the losing side. From his very humble beginnings, losing wasn't an option for Luis; he always wanted to win, to be the best, even in those early days on the streets of El Salto. The dream was simple and it came with a burning desire from within: that one day he would head to Montevideo, the capital of Uruguay 300 miles away, and star for Nacional or Peñarol, the two teams all the boys had heard fabled stories about – the two teams which had long dominated the country's club football. And the ultimate dream for Luis was that one day he would represent his country in the World Cup and bring it home on a tidal wave of adulation.

It was a dream shared at the same time by another boy in another neighbourhood in El Salto: Edinson Cavani, who was also born there. His and Luis's paths would not cross as youngsters but they now make up their country's recognised strike force. Amazingly, Cavani was born only a fortnight after Luis and just down the road in El Salto. Serendipity, maybe, but it's quite remarkable that the two men who now carry the hopes of a nation would share such a humble start in life – at the same time and in the same place.

Yes, football was a beacon of hope for young Luis and his friends – and, no doubt, just a few blocks away, for Cavani too. It was the promised land, a land where they could escape the tough streets and become somebody; it offered a way out of the poverty and slums that blighted the neighbourhood in which they were growing up: the neighbourhood Luis would call home for the first six years of his life.

Luis Alberto Suarez Diaz was born in El Salto on 24 January 1987. It was in this deprived town in the north of the country that the story of the man who would become one of the world's most feared football strikers began. He was the fourth of seven brothers, born to Rodolfo and his wife Sandra. The family were poor; they just about got by on the slim wages Rodolfo brought home from his job as a porter. Sandra stayed at home to bring up and care for their children; a housewife and mother who would always encourage Luis to make the best of his natural talents with a football. Soon Luis was proving just how talented he was after his older brother Paolo invited him along for a game with his friends. Even among older boys, Luis was still the star, the boy who could dribble with the ball as if it were glued to his right foot and who would always score the most goals.

El Salto is near to the border with Argentina and Luis and his family lived close to the army garrison in the town. 'We were only about a hundred yards away from it,' Paolo said. 'We would meet up near the camp to play football. Our routine was to get up early and spend all day outside with the ball. We went home to eat when there was food at home, and there wasn't always.'

When Luis was six, the family moved 300 miles south to Montevideo. It should have been a moment of joy for the boy, who had long dreamed of playing for one of the big clubs in the capital. There was also the bonus that both his parents

3

had now secured work – his father in a biscuit factory and his mother as a cleaner in the city's central bus station. But Luis found himself suddenly homesick for El Salto – he missed his friends and the football matches they would play at all hours of the day.

His father told him not to look back; that he would make new friends and that he would find him a junior football club where he could play the game more seriously, with a proper kit and competitive matches. But Luis would not be appeased and so Rodolfo allowed him to return to El Salto for a month to live with his grandmother, on the condition that he would come back to Montevideo with no arguing when the four-week spell was up.

Luis agreed and returned to play with his friends, reluctantly heading back to the new family home in the capital when the month ended. He would eventually settle in his new surroundings but still insisted on going back to his grandparents' house in El Salto every summer holiday for a couple of years. In his last full year in El Salto, he and his mates had swapped playing in the street for playing on a patch of land adjacent to the military base. He would now play barefoot on the grass – it would be another development in his footballing skills.

Without shoes he became even more adept at controlling the ball: now it would truly appear as if the ball were glued to his foot. He explained his homesickness for El Salto to journalist-cum-author Ana Laura Lissardy in this way: 'The change of city, the way of talking – because they talk differently there and of course they make fun of you. We came to a city where it was practically impossible to play barefoot on the grass. Of course I was going to miss it. But we had to get used to all of that as best we could.'

The point about being made fun of is a telling one. Luis would go to school like all his siblings but never felt at home. He would be teased about his protruding teeth and about being poor. It would be the start of his defiant streak: at first he would take the abuse and cry because his father had warned him not to get into any trouble. But soon he would lash out at his tormentors and get into scraps and scrapes. Luis the rebel was born; he had tried his best to keep schtum as his father had demanded but no more. No more would he be tormented and laughed at: now he would hit back and soon the bullying would end. His tormentors knew what they would get if they dared try it on with him.

But while Luis had put distance between himself and the bullies, he still found it hard to settle down to schoolwork. His educational achievements would be minimal but he consoled himself – and told his mother and father – that, no matter, he was going to be a world-famous footballer. Neither laughed at him and neither tried to talk him out of his dream. Rodolfo had been a fair footballer himself, even playing a few matches for El Salto, and his grandfather had played for Nacional. So those times when Rodolfo had told friends when they visited in El Salto, 'Well, he was born to be a footballer,' weren't as crazy as they may have initially sounded. No, Rodolfo knew something they didn't know: that football ran in the family's DNA.

At last, Luis started to settle down in his new life in

Montevideo. He began to play for a junior football team – Urreta – and made new friends. It was a team with history: the current Uruguayan international centre-half, Diego Lugano, who played for West Bromwich Albion, also starred for the youngsters six years before Luis arrived on the scene.

'When we came to live in Montevideo, we started to look for a team for him,' explains Luis's mother. 'I was told about Urreta, a club where there were a lot of people with money, so I took him there. He was sub in a friendly match a few days later. They were losing 2–0 so they put Luis on and he scored three to make it 3–2!'

Luis Suarez had made his first statement of intent at a team that meant something in his native Uruguay – a boys' team maybe but a boys' team with a strong background; one that had already seen the aforementioned Lugano move swiftly up the ladder towards the pro game. And Luis knew all about Lugano and wanted to follow in his footsteps. All he had to do now was keep on delivering the goods. He had got off to a flier and more was to follow… and quickly. The goals continued to flow and his reputation soared.

Luis would say later,

I had a really hard time when I was growing up. As you can imagine, coming from a large family, we did not have many resources at home, which meant we had to carry on with a very normal life, full of sacrifices. When I was six or seven I moved to Montevideo, where my football career began. That was the first big change in my life, and since then I have faced many other big changes. I started

playing football when I was very young and by the age
of four I would run faster with the ball than without it.

It was no real surprise when, within a couple of years of
playing for Uretta, Luis was spotted by a scout from Nacional.
Wilson Pirez was one of the most trusted scouts of the nation's
most decorated club so, when he told his bosses that he had
found a rare talent, they immediately arranged to watch him
themselves. They would not be disappointed: Luis scored
again for Uretta and was the best player on the pitch by a mile.
'I found him when he was nine, playing kids' football,' Pirez
said. 'He had an incredible amount of ability for someone of
that age. He was a wonderful boy, well behaved. You could
always tell he was going to be a great player.'

Luis was now taken under the wing of Nacional; playing
for them as a junior and having his progress monitored. It
seemed he was on the brink of a big breakthrough – but, just
as suddenly, his world fell apart when his parents split up. His
father left the family home and his mother now had to bring
him and his brothers up on little income. Luis said, 'They were
tough times. My parents had split up and there was all the
problem of us being a family that never had the possibility of
choosing anything. I was never able to tell my mother, "I want
these trainers," and have her buy me those trainers. It was the
pure reality.'

By the age of eleven he was still progressing at Nacional
but it was telling that he had to turn down an invite from
the national club to attend a national youth training camp
in Argentina because his mother could not afford to buy the

boots he needed for the trip. 'All my dreams had come true but it was too expensive so I had to decline because I didn't even have enough money to buy a pair of shoes,' he said.

It was after this setback that the stark realisation that his parents had split for good now hit him hard. Luis started to go off the rails, missing training, missing school and preferring to go to dances with his mates. He would explain what happened in this way: 'Family life was very hard because of my parents breaking up. It was hard to concentrate and I quit football.'

His brother Paolo would eventually bring him to his senses and persuade him to go back to Nacional and knuckle down. 'I knew that he was a great player and I was so mad to see him waste his talent,' Paolo explained. Luis now appeared for the club at all youth levels, scoring goals whenever and wherever he played. He worked at his football whenever he wasn't at school and also did his best to achieve some educational success when he was in the classroom. At home at night, he would study his subjects and prove more than competent in one in particular: Mathematics.

By the age of fourteen he had earned a reputation as a goal-scorer with Nacional and was well on the way to a big future with the club. But then he veered off course for the second time, partying and underage drinking. One night he was seen out on the town by club officials and the next day he was called in to see the Nacional youth-team coach, Ricardo Perdomo.

Luis was stunned when the coach grabbed him and shook him. 'You start to train properly and focus on your football – or you are out of this club!' Perdomo is said to have told him. Luis would later tell Ana Laura Lissardy, 'I went through a phase in which the football wasn't going well for me and I didn't want to study. I didn't like to train. I only liked playing the games and that way it was going to be very difficult for me to achieve something. I got really angry. I was a rebel and that worked against me.'

He would later admit, 'There were many problems... but I realised that soccer was my thing and, if I didn't give myself that chance at fourteen, I was not going to do it anymore.'

Soon it was time for Nacional to decide which youths they would keep on and groom for the future and which ones they would show the door to. Luis was one of the latter, much to his dismay. Daniel Enriquez, who was Nacional's technical director and in overall charge of the youth teams, felt the boy's attitude hadn't been good enough over the previous twelve months and told Luis's early mentor Wilson Pirez as much.

Pirez pleaded with Enriquez to give Suarez another chance. He explained that the boy had recently turned over a new leaf; that he was now buckling down to training and taking his chance very seriously indeed; that his days of late nights and partying were now over. He also pointed out that Luis was 'one of the best prospects I have ever seen' and arguably the best of all the youth players.

'Please give him one final chance,' Pirez asked. 'And if he messes up, fair enough, that's it.'

Enriquez looked at the scout who was now staking his reputation on this wayward boy Suarez, stroked his chin for a couple of minutes and then said simply, 'OK. But this is his final chance – his final warning.'

Pirez thanked him profusely and promised Enriquez he wouldn't regret the gamble he had taken. He predicted that Suarez would become a great footballer and would even represent his country one day. Enriquez nodded: he knew the boy must be something special if someone like Pirez was so willing to stick his neck out for him; to put his own reputation on the line. But Enriquez would keep an eye on the boy – and if he did step out of line, that was it: '*No mas.*'

Pirez relayed the news to Luis but warned him that this was it – it was make-or-break time and, if he didn't show sufficient dedication, commitment and progress, he would be out on his backside. Luis realised he owed much to this man and thanked him sincerely. 'I promise I won't let you down,' he told Pirez. 'From now on, football will come first. I promise you that, Mr Pirez.'

Previously, Luis had been struggling to even make the youth team as he went off the rails, but now, armed with a new determination not to let Mr Pirez down and to make the best use of his God-given talent, he became a regular. Not just a regular, mind you: he also became the kingpin of the team – the key man who could always be relied upon to score goals when they were most needed. In one match, the Nacional youth team won 21–0 – and Luis scored 17 of the goals. His team-mates grew to love him and were willing to ignore his occasional rushes of blood. Conejito, as they nicknamed him – 'Bunny' because his protruding front teeth made them think of Bugs Bunny – would score the goals that made their team formidable. And that was what mattered after all is said and done.

But it wasn't all plain sailing. Luis did keep his promise to Pirez that he would do everything he could to become a top footballer but he would continue to have problems with his temper. He was becoming a brilliant player and a model trainer, but when he saw red, there was nothing anyone could do to stop him acting up. It would be a trait that would plague him throughout his career. At the time, of course, no one thought of anger management or therapy: he was simply viewed as a hothead.

And what a hothead he could be – even at fifteen. Daniel Enriquez apparently related the story of how Luis had butted a referee at that age when he disagreed with one of his decisions in a key match. In Uruguay, Enriquez was quoted as saying, 'The referee had a broken nose and was bleeding like a cow. We punished Luis heavily and told him it was the end.'

But once again Suarez would escape the axe: Nacional had come to realise that he was a one-off; a genius who would soon enough be competing for a first-team place. So they gave him one more 'final' warning. No way were they going to kick out a boy who could score goals with ease and who could well be the one who would lead them to the league title in a season or two. No, he was far too precious for that – and if, eventually, he did prove unmanageable, well, they could sell him off for a decent fee. Business, as always, played a part in football: money talked and Luis Suarez was clearly going to be a man who would eventually make Nacional a lot of money, whether he stayed or departed.

Nacional's decision to stand by him – seemingly whatever he did – soon paid the dividends they had anticipated. Within a year, at the tender age of sixteen, Luis Suarez was knocking on the door of the first team. He trained with the first-team squad and learned from the big names in the team. His own hero had always been Argentinian legend Gabriel Batistuta. The prolific striker played most of his club football at Fiorentina in Italy and became the tenth top scorer of all-time in the Italian Serie A league, with 184 goals in 318 matches. He was Argentina's all-time leading goal-scorer, with 56 goals in 78 matches and represented his country at 3 World Cups.

This was the kind of man Luis wanted to emulate: even at the age of fifteen he knew he wanted to become a football great, someone who would go down in the annals of footballing history like Batistuta. In 1999 the Argentine had come third in the FIFA World Player of the Year awards and Luis was keen to make the record books himself – only he wanted to win the Player of the Year award itself! Luis was also impressed by one particular tribute paid to Batistuta – the one from Diego Maradona, who had said Batistuta was simply the best striker he had ever seen.

In Luis's eyes, that really was something. He knew Maradona was arguably the greatest player ever, despite his shortcomings, and to receive such words of praise from such a legendary fellow professional truly meant something. Despite his short temper and apparent inherently selfish nature, Luis Suarez DID care what people said about him: especially those he played with and those he played against. He never deliberately set out to hurt an opponent and, invariably, he ended up full of self-reproach and self-hatred when he came to terms with the consequences of his lack of self-control. And he too would pay a price when the red mist descended. He would wish he could turn back the clock but was at a loss to know how to stop acting up as he did. Only after a couple of years at Liverpool did he finally get help with his temper; only then did he learn there were ways to deal with the black dog that drove him to acts that he would deeply regret.

As a teenager he had been taught the idea that 'we are all big boys here' and that he should simply 'pull himself together' when he acted out of line. It would be many years before someone – namely Liverpool's wonderful human being of a manager Brendan Rodgers – would tell him he could get help to change; that there were people who could teach him how to deal with things differently and how to avoid the confrontations that had so scarred his otherwise brilliant career.

But as a fifteen-year-old playing in Uruguay at the time, no such help was offered. He was a boy with a problem temperament playing among men who had no inclination to help a kid who was clearly struggling to keep his emotions in check. Luckily, Luis did come across someone who could and did help calm him. She would become the most important person in his life and influence on his career – and on his eventual move away from his homeland to Europe. Her name was Sofia Balbi and they would eventually marry and have children.

Luis was fifteen when he met Sofia, then twelve, in Montevideo. He told her he was a footballer and treated her with respect, mindful of her age. She, in turn, told her parents about him and they welcomed him, initially with a certain wariness, given he was a footballer, but they grew to like him and encouraged him to visit their daughter whenever he had any free time. They felt they could trust Luis and saw him as a gentle boy. Away from the football field, he was a totally different character; somewhat shy, diffident even, and certainly not someone who was full of himself and aggressive (as he could be when in the colours of Nacional).

And Sofia could get through to him like no one else. Young she may have been but she cared enough for him to see he was essentially a boy who had a lot of pain inside – a boy who had issues but had never talked about them. Sofia encouraged him to speak about his feelings and he felt an unusual calmness in her company. She also encouraged him to work hard at school – telling him that he was no dunce – and to give his best on the training and football pitches.

Her influence could be seen as he started to do better at school and became a prolific goal machine for Nacional's youth team. 'I began to score goals,' he would later say. 'And I got to the point where I almost broke the Nacional youth record. The record was 64 goals in a full year and I scored 63. Things like that gave you confidence.'

The relationship between Luis and Sofia developed and he realised this girl was much more than just his first sweetheart: he instinctively knew she would be his first and LAST sweetheart. He knew from way back then that this was the girl he would marry; she made him feel good and made him feel calm. She was the steadying personal influence on his life that had been missing since the break-up of his parents' marriage.

But then, from out of nowhere, Luis would suffer yet

another of those out-of-the-blue setbacks that had knocked him sidewards over the years – the family move from his beloved El Salto to Montevideo, his parents' break-up and now the departure from his life of the young girl who had so affected him for the better over the previous year.

One night, when he arrived at Sofia's home after football training, he found her with tears in her eyes, unable to talk. 'What is up?' Luis asked, deeply concerned. 'We are leaving Montevideo,' she finally told him, tears running down her face. 'We are going to live in Spain – in Barcelona.'

Luis – who by now had also earned the nickname 'The Gunner' from his team-mates, courtesy of his ability to gun teams down with his goals – sighed and did his best to hold back his own tears. 'Don't worry,' he eventually managed, tears now streaking down his face. 'It is not the end. I will become a great player and will score so many goals that Barcelona will want to sign me! Then we will be together again.'

Sofia would later admit, 'The day before we moved, I will never forget. Me and Luis went for a walk and sat at a bus stop and we both started to cry. I couldn't stop because I did not think we would see each other again.'

But Luis had other ideas. He was determined that they would be together and he meant what he'd said about joining Barcelona (he had always dreamed that he would eventually play for the Catalan giants). Luis Suarez now had a catalyst to get into the Nacional first team and to become a renowned goal-scorer. For if he did so, he would earn the move that would reunite him with his sweetheart. And when Luis puts his mind to something, he ALWAYS achieves it. Soon he would take the first step towards that reunion by making it into the Nacional first team at the tender age of seventeen.

CHAPTER TWO

OPENING SHOTS

With his sweetheart Sofia now in Barcelona starting a new life for her and her family, Luis Suarez was left to pick up the pieces of his fractured romance back in Montevideo. He remained determined to reunite with Sofia and they kept in touch via email and telephone. Luis learned that Sofia liked Barcelona – although, of course, she didn't like it one bit being apart from him. She told him how wonderful and vibrant a city the Catalan capital was and how he would love it too; how it was full of life and how its people seemed to love life and lived it to the full. Sofia was also full of enthusiasm about the city's love of football and how the public loved FC Barcelona. 'The people seemed obsessed with the football club,' a friend of the couple said. 'Everywhere Sofia went, there were people talking about FC Barca this, FC Barca that. It was clearly a football-crazy city and she just knew that Luis would love the place. He had always fancied the idea of playing for a major European team and now he had one to aim for: Barcelona. It became his dream to play for them – and to get back with Sofia and make a home there.'

That dream and love of everything Barca never left Luis, I am told by a source close to him. Even now he still loves Liverpool and the fans who have stood by him through thick and thin. But given the chance to play for another team in Europe, his choice, I am reliably informed, was always to turn out for the giants of the Camp Nou. And it all dates back to those days when he and Sofia were forced apart.

The one upside to Sofia's departure was that it now encouraged Luis to devote himself completely to the Nacional cause. He may have been lovelorn and sad that she had gone but he had that overriding aim: to be such a success that he would earn the move to Europe that would enable him to reunite with his girl. Now he could concentrate 100 per cent on his football, with no distractions. The days of wine, women and partying were truly over for Luis: he was committed to his absent love and to his career. He was a boy with a mission and his dedication would surely mean he would achieve his number-one aim swiftly.

But it didn't quite work out that way. True, he did devote all his efforts to football but, for all his talent and dedication, he appeared to struggle when he finally made the first team. Luis was overjoyed when the coach told him he was in for his full debut, at the age of eighteen, but he found it difficult to get among the goals.

Luis would start for the first time for the Montevideo giants on 3 May 2005, against Junior de Barranquilla in the Libertadores Cup. Yet he would not get that all-important first goal until 10 September 2005. He certainly had the talent and the confidence, yet the boy who couldn't stop scoring throughout his youth career and burgeoning semi-pro career had now hit a barren streak. He would frequently return home with his head low and slump into an armchair in front of the television. His mother would do her best to encourage and cajole him but he would shrug his shoulders and say he 'had lost his touch in front of goal' and that he was worried he might never recover it.

Maybe it was the absence of his girlfriend that was affecting his confidence – or maybe he was putting himself under too much pressure to deliver. Long after he finally hit his first goal for Nacional, Luis would say that he was at a loss to explain why it had taken him so long to end his goal drought. He was just relieved that it was over and grateful to the head coach who had stood by him during those hellish sixteen weeks.

Martin Lasarte had been under enormous pressure from fans to drop Luis during that difficult start to his first-team career in 2005. He watched in horror as the teenager fluffed chance after chance. But he also retained his belief in the boy; he believed that Luis had the potential to become a world-class striker and felt that axing him from the team would ruin his confidence and set him back in his career. Lasarte would remain steadfast that Suarez should play on until he finally broke his goal-scoring duck. He stood by him as the fans made clear their discontent week after week.

Lasarte had seen Luis at work on the training ground and never had any doubt he could deliver the goals that would make Nacional real contenders for the league title. And, much to his own delight and credit, he would eventually be proved right. For when Luis broke his duck, the goals would come regularly and the fans would take him to heart. They knew they had a forward of exceptional ability and, after months of demanding his head, they now praised him and prayed the club would keep him.

Lasarte, now aged fifty-three, would remember the days of trouble and toil with a shake of the head and a wry smile. He told journalist Mike McGrath that he never even contemplated taking Luis out of the team. Lasarte said, 'It was difficult for some people to accept but I couldn't think like that as I had trust in him and still saw that potential in him. It was tough to take it but I kept playing him in games until we were able to see what he could do. And in the end it was worth it.'

Lasarte's trust in Luis led to Nacional winning the Uruguayan Primera Division title in the 2005–06 season. From flop to hero, Suarez's debut season in the big-time would certainly be one he would never forget. His ten goals in twenty-seven games were a key part of that championship-winning run.

Lasarte explained just why he had stood by Luis:

That talent and ambition was always in Luis so, if I didn't stick with him, another coach or team would have seen it. That is the same today as it was then. It was important to me as a coach to make that decision. The trust I had in him was important and he has said that himself. I remember that as soon as Luis scored his first goal he carried the responsibility of a great player. It was like he was older than he actually was. He carried that responsibility – the team were the champions and he was the leader of them, despite his age. He was one of the best players that I have trained and was definitely the best I ever gave a debut to. It was not only his talent and the physical qualities that everyone could see, his will to win was also important.

But now Lasarte's worst fears would materialise. He had always believed Luis would go to the very top of his trade but had anticipated having him at his disposal for at least three or four seasons. Lasarte planned to build on the league-title winning success and develop a team that would go down in the annals of history at Nacional. He wanted to create a team that would compare with the best ever – and Luis certainly played a vital role in that dream.

Yet just twelve months after Luis had helped Nacional to the league crown, he was gone – away to Europe and back into the arms of Sofia. Well, at least back with her more regularly than he had been in Uruguay. For when Europe came calling for Luis Suarez, it wasn't the men from Barcelona who came knocking at the door.

Instead, it would be representatives from the Netherlands who saw the potential in the boy from El Salto. But again, it would be a surprise. You may have expected giants of Dutch football, such as Ajax Amsterdam or PSV Eindhoven or Feyenoord, to want to sign Luis. But, no, it would be the manager of the relatively little-known Groningen who arrived at Nacional with a cheque book and who refused to take 'no' for an answer.

I was told,

Lasarte had always feared that other clubs would want to sign Luis when they saw him in action – when he started knocking the goals in regularly. But the Nacional coach never for one moment imagined it would be a smaller club who would come in for his boy. He certainly believed Luis was good enough to play for Barcelona, Real Madrid or even Liverpool or Chelsea. He was shocked when the boy signed for Groningen. And who can blame him? No one connected with Nacional expected their number-one talent to leave for a club that was arguably not even as big as the one he was already playing for in Montevideo.

To give the talent spotters from Groningen their due, they certainly could spot ability when they saw it. They had, in fact, travelled to watch another player in a match that took place the day before Nacional's match against rivals Defensor. They only attended the Nacional game as they were at a loose end on the Sunday. But as they looked on, they quickly realised they were watching someone special. That day Luis converted a penalty and scored a fabulous solo goal which led to a team win. His display left the talent scouts mesmerised and they swiftly forgot all about signing the man they had travelled all that way to see, deciding almost immediately that Suarez was the man for them.

They approached him and told him as much – and he didn't take much convincing. OK, this wasn't Barcelona he would be moving to but it was a team in Europe and that would take him much closer to being back with Sofia. And the Netherlands wasn't that far away from Barca anyway, well, was it? Groningen offered Nacional a fee of around €800,000 (then around £500,000), which they gladly accepted.

Luis would later admit, 'When the call came from Europe, I didn't think twice. The first thing that came to mind was being near Sofia.'

As part of the deal, it was agreed that Luis would see the season out at Nacional and only then would he embark on his journey to Europe.

Luis would later recall the day he played his way to a transfer in this way, when speaking to the *Daily Mail*: 'It was the best game I ever had in Uruguay! The way I beat those players for my goal I did exactly as I intended to do. They [the Groningen scouts] were in Uruguay to see a different player from a different team. But they'd watched him on the Saturday and then chosen to watch our game on the Sunday. Afterwards they talked to me, and then told me they wanted to buy me. After one game.'

Luis was only nineteen when he finally left Montevideo for FC Groningen. In his time at the Dutch club, he would score eleven goals in thirty-three matches. His mother was sad but told him he was making the right decision; that he would get closer to his ambition of becoming one of the world's best footballers as the spotlight would be on him much more in Europe than it had been in Uruguay. She was also pleased he would be closer to Sofia as she knew how much the girl meant to her boy. As she waved him off at the airport in the summer of 2006, she had a tear in her eye but Sandra Suarez has always known her son was destined for greatness and this was merely another step on that journey.

Luis was also in more regular contact with his father Rodolfo by now and he, too, encouraged him to make the move. A fine footballer himself at a lesser level, Rodolfo would support his son as he moved onwards and upwards and the two would have a closer relationship as the years rolled by. Rodolfo was determined to build bridges; to make amends after walking out on the family when Luis was younger. Luis, for his part, was a very forgiving person and was glad to have his father back in his life in a bigger way.

Daniel Rosa, who worked in the media department of Nacional, said there had been a time when it looked as if Luis might fall by the wayside as a footballer – after he had to leave El Salto for Montevideo and when his parents split up – and he credited Luis's mentor Wilson Pirez with convincing him that everything would work out OK and that he should continue to pursue his footballing dream.

Rosa said, 'He was missing his family and wanted to go back to Salto. Wilson was one of the people who cared about him and was by his side. He did everything he could to try to get him to stay in Montevideo. Wilson was very important. That is why he has very good memories of Wilson and speaks so highly of him. It was a difficult moment and he was in trouble. But Wilson helped him to focus on football.'

Nowadays Luis looks back on that time in a much more

relaxed frame of mind and admits his father has played an important role in his development as a footballer, that they still speak regularly and that any rift from those early days in Montevideo has long healed. Indeed, Luis recently joked, 'I wasn't even the best player in my house. I am one of six children and two of my brothers [Paolo and Max] are footballers too. And my father Rodolfo was a footballer. My parents separated when I was nine but my father was always around and he still follows me now. He is always sending me messages.'

Luis would take time to settle into his new surroundings in the Netherlands, although he looked forward to playing in the Dutch league and experiencing a different continent's approach to the game. Groningen was the largest city in the north of the Netherlands and was recognised as a civilised place, home to 25,000 university students and a centre of culture. Friends of Luis's would say it 'didn't have the rough edges of Montevideo' and there was a certain truth in that. It was home to several museums and theatres and its nightlife was much dictated by the whims of the students from its two universities. 'Basically, it was a nice place – but a little bit dull in comparison to Montevideo and Luis needed time to settle down as life was lived at a much slower pace in the city and at the football club,' I was told.

Luis initially found the language barrier a problem but was determined to learn Dutch. He was aided by fellow Uruguayan Bruno Silva, who was already playing at Groningen. Silva helped him settle in the city and adapt to the different way of life. They would soon become firm friends and Luis would say how grateful he was to Silva for taking the time and effort to ameliorate his arrival in a strange place.

It also didn't take long for Luis to travel to Spain to see Sofia. He admitted, 'I was still a child when I arrived in Holland. Everything was new, everything was strange but I was going to give it my best shot. When I signed the contract, I had twelve days off and went to Barcelona because Sofia was there, and she showed me around.'

Groningen FC was like the city: safe, stable and a nice place to be. It was never going to be like playing for Ajax with that club's fanatical supporters but it was a good staging post for Luis Suarez as he found his feet in Europe after moving from South America. The club would also never be a major European player but it had its moments. Luis made his debut in August 2006 in the home match against Feyenoord, which Groningen won 3–0. He only came on as an 88th-minute substitute but at least it gave him a feel for his new footballing environment.

When Luis arrived, the team had qualified for the UEFA Cup and he scored for them in their first-round tie against Partizan Belgrade in September 2006. It would be his first goal in the European competition but would not be enough to stop Groningen crashing out at an early stage. They lost 4–2 in the first leg in Belgrade, with Luis grabbing their second goal two minutes into injury time. The Dutch team won the return leg a fortnight later 1–0 but it was still not enough to save them from an early exit.

Luis proved he could score goals anywhere as he now hit the back of the net regularly for the Dutch outfit. But the red mist that had first appeared back when he was playing in Uruguay again descended upon him as he starred for Groningen. The disciplinary worries that had scarred his career even in his early teens now reared their ugly head in his first season in the Netherlands. In January 2007, for example, he would score four times but also collected three yellow cards and one red. The following month he would also be dismissed when playing for his country. It was a stain on his career but would become something of a regular occurrence and it would be the one thing thrown at him over the years as he proved himself as good a striker as anyone in world football: that his genius came with an unfortunate notoriety because he could not control his temper. It would only be in 2014, after Liverpool boss Brendan Rodgers took him under his wing and told him he needed to change his ways – to control his anger – that the problem finally appeared to be eliminated. Luis would be twenty-seven years of age before the penny finally dropped: that he didn't need to resort to temper tantrums as he was now arguably the best forward in the world. But then, of course, would come his bit on Chiellini in the World Cup – and he was back at square one after all Rodgers's efforts to help him.

A year after signing for Groningen, Luis was gone – and this time he would go in style, signing for the biggest club in Holland and one of the most recognisable names in club football in Europe. He had enjoyed his time at Groningen and his burgeoning partnership with fellow striker Erik Nevland (who was once on Manchester United's books). But the call of Ajax in Amsterdam was too powerful to resist. It had always been his dream to play for the world's most famous clubs and a move to Amsterdam was a big staging post on that journey. Sports historians had marked out the club's claim to fame, saying it was the seventh most successful European club of the twentieth century. But Groningen were displeased at the prospect of losing a player of such potential and laughed off Ajax's initial valuation of €3.5 million. Luis made it clear he wanted to move and threatened to go to the Dutch League's arbitration committee unless Groningen agreed to him moving on. Groningen stood firm and watched as Luis carried out his threat but the committee ruled against him and he left the hearing confused and worried. It would be difficult to return to Groningen after his court move – the fans would hardly be on his side after he had made such a desperate attempt to escape them and the club.

It was then that Ajax returned with a solution agreeable to all, more than doubling their offer to €7.5 million. Groningen still didn't appreciate the way they were being manipulated to sell their star man but they, too, realised this was the end of the road. There was no point in keeping an unhappy player and, anyway, the offer was now acceptable. So they let Luis go. He left the club with some fond memories of his time there but was happier still that his efforts to quit had paid off and that he could now pursue his dream of greater success with a bigger club. It is interesting to note how, six years later, he would try a similar tactic to exit Liverpool for what he believed was a move that would lead him to a bigger club and bigger money. The only difference was that Liverpool would not be persuaded by his clumsy attempts to leave: they were, after all, already one of the biggest clubs in the world, unlike little Groningen.

But for now, in the summer of 2007, Luis Suarez was about to join the third club of his burgeoning professional career – and the biggest yet. Yes, he was off to Amsterdam to become an idol at Ajax.

CHAPTER THREE

THE KING OF AMSTERDAM

Luis arrived in Amsterdam to much acclaim in the summer of 2007. The Ajax supporters are renowned for their fanaticism and loyalty to their club – they are among the most enthusiastic and noisiest fans in Europe. They follow their club all over the place and, like Liverpool fans, expect their team to play with passion and skill but, most of all, with creativity and artistry. They are fans who have been brought up with some of the most individually talented players ever in world football. The likes of the legendary Marco van Basten, Dennis Bergkamp and Johan Cruyff have treated them to moments of skill and joy that they will cherish for ever.

So they turned out in their thousands to welcome Luis Suarez when he arrived at the Amsterdam Arena in August 2007 for his unveiling as an Ajax player. They had heard all about the boy from Uruguay and seen him in action first hand

and on their TV screens as he blitzed the goals for Groningen. They recognised him immediately as one of their own – a man whose passion and commitment to the cause shone through and someone who could perhaps reach the dizzy heights of their former heroes. They were convinced that in Suarez they had signed a footballer who had it in him to become not just a star in Amsterdam and the Netherlands but who could become one of the biggest names in European and world football.

And, tantalisingly, someone who might – just might – put Ajax back on the map as a European footballing superpower after years of underachieving in the continent's competitions. Their last European Cup win was in 1995 and their last UEFA Cup win five years earlier. The club had moved into a brand-new, sparkling home in 1996 – the Amsterdam Arena – but star players were continually being sold off and, by the dawn of the new millennium, Ajax were struggling to replicate their European successes of earlier years.

Yet still the fan base remained strong and boisterous. The Arena stadium can hold 52,000 people and the average attendance in 2006–07 was 48,610, rising in the season of Luis's arrival to 49,128. So Luis knew he now had the mass audience he had always craved: a full house of around 50,000 fans who would adore him if he turned it on regularly. At this stage of his career, still only twenty years old, he had found an ideal place to call home. He knew from his year at Groningen that he could easily excel and stand out as a star; perhaps the biggest star in the Dutch Premier League, known as the Eredivisie.

Ajax announced his arrival on 9 August with the following press statement:

Ajax and FC Groningen have reached agreement about the immediate transfer of Luis Suarez to Ajax. The forward from Uruguay signs a five-year contract in Amsterdam. Suarez still has to undergo a medical examination. Ajax pay a direct fee of €7.5 million for the player. Twenty-year-old Suarez played for FC Groningen last season. There, he scored 10 goals in 29 league matches. Before that he played for Nacional in Uruguay. Also because of the long and historic relationship between FC Groningen and Ajax the clubs have been in continuous dialogue during the whole process, which has led to this positive result.

Luis himself said how proud he was to have joined a world-famous club in Europe after his humble beginnings in a poor district of El Salto. 'When I look back and think of all the friends in the neighbourhood in those half-ruined, dusty soccer fields on the streets of Montevideo where I played with a football, I feel very proud.'

But Luis's debut for his new club would not come before 50,000 adoring fans in Amsterdam: instead he would make his bow in the Dutch Cup away against an amateur team. Kozakken Boys play in a 5,000-capacity ground in Werkendam, a town in the south of the Netherlands, and the arrival of the biggest club in the country stirred imaginations. The event on the day – 26 September 2007 – was a sell-out as the locals dreamed of beating Ajax and making it into the third round of the Cup. Inevitably, that dream was short-lived but the amateurs still gave Ajax plenty to think about and far from disgraced themselves. The Amsterdam giants won 2–1 and Luis made an impressive start to his time with the club.

It was interesting to note the names of some of his team-mates from that day – men who, like Luis, would go on to forge a name for themselves in England. Men such as Johnny Heitinga, the central defender who scored from the penalty spot to put Ajax ahead, and who would eventually play for Everton and Fulham; and Jan Vertonghen, another classy defender, who would end up at Tottenham. Yes, Luis was in good company as he began his career at Ajax with a win.

In his first campaign with the club he scored twenty-two goals in forty-four games – a goal every other game – and that record and his obvious natural ability and keenness to win every ball and be the best made him a big favourite with the Ajax fans. He also had that essential ingredient that all the best strikers possess: an innate selfishness to claim every goal and all the glory. It meant that some of his team-mates were not as happy with him as the fans but then they did have the consolation of winning more games when Luis was in the side because of his constant torrent of goals.

Another factor in his favour was his genuine willingness to learn from his managers and coaches. He was lucky at Ajax to work with a selection of the best – Marco van Basten, Dennis Bergkamp, Frank de Boer, Henk ten Cate and Martin Jol. Luis would later admit,

Even as a kid in Uruguay I knew I would one day have to play in Europe. And I saw Holland as a great school.

I learned so much in my time in Holland and, because of the way they do things there, I don't think I would have learned as much somewhere else. I was a selfish player. But they taught me the importance of being part of a team. Van Basten taught me a lot about how to play as a forward; about shooting techniques and about things that worked for him. His movement, his technique. And from all of them I learned about remaining calm on the pitch; when in front of goal and also when being fouled. You have to try not to react; take a step back. I learned to control my attitude more.

His first season at Ajax saw him settle in and earn that one-in-two-game goal-scoring ratio and his goals helped the team finish runners-up in the league. During the next campaign – 2008–09 – he continued to improve and excel, to such an extent that the Ajax fans chose him as their Player of the Year. His manager during the season was Dutch legend Van Basten. The former striker admitted that Luis's twenty-two goals in thirty-one league games had played a key role in helping the team finish third in the table. But Van Basten also expressed dismay about Suarez's discipline, saying he picked up far too many yellow cards.

In one match for Ajax, Luis was involved in a half-time punch-up with team-mate Albert Luque over a free-kick routine that went wrong. It was a punch-up that led to Van Basten himself suspending Luis. 'He is unpredictable and hard to influence, but that makes him special too,' a clearly bemused Van Basten would say by way of explanation for the ban.

Luis admired Van Basten for his exploits as a player of supreme quality and had no real problem with his attitude towards him as his manager at Ajax. He was intelligent enough to realise that Marco had to show, in public at least, that he was the man in charge at the club; that he, Luis, could not expect to get away with unacceptable behaviour simply because he was rapidly emerging as the team's star man.

Van Basten would leave his post in 2009. The new man at the helm was a big fan of Luis so Ajax's star player was delighted to welcome Big Martin Jol as his new manager. Jol immediately boosted his confidence by telling him he was going to be his key man and backed it up by making him club captain within a fortnight of taking over from Van Basten. The vacancy had arisen when stalwart centre-half Thomas Vermaelen left Ajax to join Arsenal in London.

Suarez rewarded Jol's faith by ending the season as the league's top scorer with thirty-five goals in thirty-three games. In total, he hit forty-nine goals in all competitions and helped Ajax lift the Dutch Cup. His goal spree meant he was not only top scorer at Ajax but also in Europe in terms of goals per games. He had started the 2009–10 season as he intended to go on with a hat-trick in a 4–1 win against RKC Waalwijk – his three goals all coming in the last twenty minutes. The striker then hit four goals per game in wins over Slovan Bratislava in the Europa League play-off round, VVV-Venlo and Roda JC Kerkrade. He grabbed another three in the first half in another win over VVV-Venlo and then found the back of the net SIX times against WHC Wezep in the Dutch Cup as Ajax won by a club-record margin of 14–1.

The 14–1 victory at the end of December put Ajax into the quarter-finals of the cup but Luis would miss out as he blotted his copybook by getting booked against WHC Wezep. It was a common denominator throughout his career – the good and the bad side by side. Ajax put out a statement praising him but also pointing out he had let the side down:

> Ajax closed 2009 in style on Wednesday night. During this round of sixteen match in the FC Zwolle stadium, the team from Amsterdam was much too strong for the amateurs from WHC: 1–14. Luis Suarez had six goals to his credit, but also received a costly yellow card. It was the only blotch on the evening – the yellow card coming midway through the first-half. The captain received yellow for comments to the referee. As he had already received a yellow card during the previous round's game against FC Dordrecht, the captain will have to sit out the quarter-finals, making his words to the referee very costly ones.

Luis had a chance at redemption in the final of the competition and, right on cue, he scored two goals in the second leg of the Cup final and finished as the tournament's top scorer. His brace was important: it would help Ajax lift the Cup as they strolled to a 6–1 aggregate win over fierce Feyenoord. It was the eighteenth time Ajax had won the trophy and Luis was proud to lift it as team captain.

However, his goals could not lift the Eredivisie trophy for Ajax – they would finish runners-up to FC Twente, coached by former England boss Steve McClaren. But Suarez was the league's top scorer with 35 goals in 33 games and 49 goals in all competitions.

His goal-scoring efforts earned him the Ajax Player of the Year for the second season in a row and the coveted Dutch Footballer of the Year trophy. Luis was particularly delighted to lift the national award for his glittering contribution to Ajax's campaign. It showed his efforts were being recognised nationwide in Holland – and this, in turn, would surely create a stir on the European continent.

He was certainly creating a real stir in the Netherlands. The Dutch magazine *Elsevier* led the way in noting just how brilliant his contribution to the nation's football had been, commenting, 'Ajax striker Luis Suarez is the best football player in Holland. He was in the lead throughout the Player of the Year voting. The Uruguayan will also soon receive the Golden Boot award as the top scorer in the Dutch league. The 23-year-old is the most prolific foreign goal-scorer EVER in the Dutch league.'

The praise was handsome and justified: Luis Suarez was the best player in the Netherlands and his exploits were now beginning to be noted in other countries. His showing at the World Cup in the summer that followed only served to increase the number of clubs from other countries who now sent their European scouts to watch him when he returned to play for Ajax in August 2010. The headlines in South Africa may have been about his handball in the match against Ghana but the subtext on his form and skill suggested that here was a player who could deliver the goods in any country, given the chances. OK, his temperament remained a problem but if you could solve that conundrum, you would have a world-class footballer on your hands.

That was certainly how one particularly interested observer viewed Luis Suarez. Yes, Kenny Dalglish may have been out of work in the summer of 2010 but he always had an eye on top-class players and if any stood out, he would mention their names to the management team at Liverpool, where he remained a club ambassador. As he followed the World Cup that summer, King Kenny's attention was drawn to the little Uruguayan. As a goal-scorer himself, he knew that Luis Suarez was a natural and he decided to keep tabs on the player when he returned from South Africa to go to Holland for the 2010–11 season with Ajax.

Of course, Ajax had no intention of selling their star man. Keeping him was part of the reasoning behind boss Martin Jol's decision to make Luis captain twelve months earlier. Jol knew he had a gifted goal-scorer and that such men were not easy to come by. Luis proved that was exactly the case soon after returning from the World Cup, by hitting his hundredth goal for Ajax as they were held 1–1 by Greek side PAOK in a Champions League qualifier at the Amsterdam Arena. It meant he was the fourteenth player ever to score more than a hundred goals for Ajax and only the third non-Dutchman to do so. As Jol saw it, his boy was notching up records and was settled in Amsterdam. He had married Sofia in March 2009 and the couple lived together in the city. They had wed in Montevideo and relatives surprised them by playing a video of them together when they were teenagers. Big name Uruguayan stars – including Diego Lugano and Alvaro Gonzalez – attended the ceremony, much to Luis's delight.

And in August 2010, as Luis was still celebrating his World Cup success and that hundredth goal, Sofia gave birth to their first child – a daughter they would name Delfina. But there had been talk that he would still move to Barcelona – that Sofia wanted to move back there – in the summer of 2010. I am told that preliminary talks did take place but that Ajax would not agree to their star player's transfer. Jol told his board that he wanted to keep Luis on board regardless of Barcelona's interest and, when asked by the press if a deal was on the cards, Jol dismissed the suggestions, saying, 'I know clubs are interested because he's scored in all competitions, forty-five goals, and even in Holland that is a great amount of goals. I don't know what will happen but he's got a high price – and I think that makes it pretty difficult for a club to afford him.'

So Luis stayed but he was not totally happy. At that time, every player dreamed of turning out for Barca, the undisputed best club side in the world and, with Sofia's love of the Catalan city and Luis's own desire to play for them, it left him feeling low when the chance of a deal faded.

It was while still smarting from the collapse of the proposed move that Luis started to make headlines for the wrong reasons and it would end up a few months later in an incident that led to him being labelled 'the Cannibal of Ajax'. The striker was seen on TV biting PSV Eindhoven midfielder Otman Bakkal during Ajax's 0–0 draw in the Eredivisie. The referee did not see the incident in injury time during the match in November

2010 and Suarez escaped punishment on the day. It happened after ref Bjorn Kuipers showed Ajax's Rasmus Lindgren a straight red for a bad tackle on Ibrahim Afellay. Suarez then argued with Bakkal, who stood on the Uruguayan's foot, prompting him to bite the PSV midfielder's shoulder.

But Luis would not escape sanctions from the league after the incident was reassessed by a video panel. It didn't help his case that prominent Dutch newspaper *De Telegraaf* gave him his new nickname and called for his club and the Dutch Football Association to take action.

Ajax immediately issued a two-match suspension on their player in the hope that it would make the Dutch FA (the KNVB) come down more lightly on the player. The move did not work.

The eyes of the world were now on the Dutch FA and they had no choice but to take action – and to act swiftly and severely. They announced that Luis would be banned for seven games. Luis and Ajax immediately accepted the sanctions and agreed that he would pay a substantial fine, which would go to charity. They then issued a joint statement, which read like this: 'Ajax and Luis Suarez have accepted the KNVB's settlement proposal of a seven-match suspension. The Ajax player received the suspension after his bite towards PSV player Otman Bakkal. In total, Suarez will be a spectator for six competition matches, and the cup match against AZ. The next competition match in which he'll play will be Ajax – De Graafschap on February 4, 2011. Ajax sanctioned its captain on Monday with a fine and a suspension for two upcoming competition matches against VVV-Venlo and NEC. The fine will go towards a charitable cause. The KNVB suspension is effective immediately.'

The striker was, however, permitted to play against AC Milan in the Champions League two weeks after the bite – if Ajax decided he was up to it. The Dutch FA's disciplinary committee would later admit they decided to come down hard on the player because they deemed the act to be 'violent'.

Luis was repentant and apologised in a video he uploaded on to his Facebook page. He said he was very embarrassed by the nature of the incident and for the bite itself and added, 'I feel very bad about biting. The worst thing is harming another person and I have apologised for what happened in Holland. It's something I regret.'

Fans around the world condemned Suarez for his behaviour. One typical comment was, 'This guy BIT a fellow human being. I know those guys that crashed in the Andes had to eat each other, but can anybody even begin to defend this "man"? (I use the term very, very loosely indeed).' While another football fan said, 'Mike Tyson was banned for way longer for the same act in boxing, which is at least considered to be a combat sport. How you can get away with a ban of just seven matches in football is beyond belief.'

Some Ajax fans rushed to defend Luis, pointing out that Bakkal had provoked him by deliberately treading on his foot. But it was difficult to feel sympathy: it was a barbaric act and one that deserved the ban and could even have earned a bigger one. And the truly depressing thing is that, even with the benefit of hindsight, Luis would not learn from his failing. No, he would go on to bite another player (Branislav

Ivanovic) when starring for Liverpool – but more on that in a later chapter.

In December 2010 Luis was granted leave by Ajax to return home to Uruguay with wife Sofia and their baby daughter, Delfina. During his time there, he spoke with the Uruguayan press pack about the bite incident and how it had affected him. He said,

What everyone saw was the big bite but not what happened during the game. I had several brushes with him [Bakkal] throughout the game and he kept stepping on me. In Holland, they showed everything he did to me in that game and why I reacted the way I did. I was very heated and I thought to myself I wasn't going [to] hit him or kick him but when I got closer to him, it just occurred to me to bite him.

It would have gone unnoticed since there was a crowd of players but the camera caught me. I never thought the repercussion would be this big. I accept that I made a mistake and that's what I publicly apologised for. It was a reaction that one shouldn't have, least of all to me, being the captain and image of this club.

I felt like I had to face my mistake head on, just like I do when things go well. I accept the consequence the club gave me and I understand it because I know I made a mistake. However, it upset me that the Dutch Football Federation gave me a too-long suspension and that the club didn't defend me. They should have understood that I am only human and wanted to defend myself but they didn't.

Luis said that he was grateful to the Ajax fans for still standing by him despite the nature of the incident: 'The first few days after the incident happened, I did not feel like going outside to the streets. I was embarrassed. I dreaded that someone would say something or that people would laugh at me. But it was the absolute contrary. The supporters sent emails that I shouldn't have to apologise and that I've always given my all for this club. Their support made me very happy.'

Luis's curtain call for Ajax would come in Milan when he appeared for the Amsterdam giants in their Champions League group match in December 2010. He would play an important role in their 2–0 win in the San Siro – a win that meant they finished third in Group G and, therefore, qualified for the last thirty-two of the Europa League. Goals from Demy de Zeeuw and Toby Alderweireld secured the win but Suarez was a constant thorn in the side for Milan, who were already assured of second place in the group.

For his final match, Luis was coached by interim boss Frank de Boer after Martin Jol resigned his post two days before the game after a poor run of form by the four-time European champions. Jol, deprived of the services of Suarez, had seen the Amsterdam club drop to fourth in the Dutch Eredivisie. 'With pain in my heart I say goodbye to this wonderful club,' said Jol. 'We started something last summer that I would have finished but I have come to realise that the expectations after last season were too high. We cannot meet such expectations. The amount of criticism that the club has had to endure daily has led to unrest in the club and among players. I take this decision consciously before AC Milan v Ajax is played. The coming weeks are very important and I sincerely hope that something happens in the squad to make it in the short term a winning team.'

Without the banned Suarez, Ajax were simply not the same team. Luis's bite had not only cost him his own place, it had also hastened his manager's exit. Luis did not know at the time that the match against PSV would be his last league game for Ajax, nor that the Milan Champions League encounter would be his last game ever for the club. But it was always going to be difficult for him to return to the club and play in the Dutch League after the outrage over his bite incident. And while talking to the Uruguayan press pack during his return home in December 2010, he made it clear that he himself believed a change of club and country would now be for the best. He said,

I would like a change of scene. I would like to be better and I'm not talking about my financial status. I want to be better in the football sense, to learn, and to show different abilities that perhaps I don't get a chance to in Dutch football.

Maybe I can go to a bigger club that has grand players that may be able to help me in many different things. Or to have a different coach that will better help me in areas that I'm having difficulty in. I would love to take that step. But these are not things that I decide. I'm very aware about how transfers work, in the winter and in the summer, it's very complicated. These days clubs pay more attention towards the marketability of a player and not so much about the quality or what a player can contribute to the game. After the World Cup I think I've improved in this area, of marketability. I just hope something happens.

And something would happen as Dame Fortune now played her part in his destiny. For just as he was sitting out his ban in Uruguay, talking to that nation's press about his hopes and dreams and wondering just what turn his future would take, Liverpool FC were busy sacking their manager, Roy Hodgson.

And the man who would now take his place was very much a confirmed admirer of Luis Suarez. Yes, Kenny Dalglish knew all about the Uruguayan after his World Cup exploits and had earmarked him as a possible Liverpool player. Now Dalglish would take to the helm at Liverpool and told the club's American owners that he wanted to make Suarez his first signing.

Luis had spent four seasons at Ajax, scoring 111 goals and leaving as an idol among the club's fans. He joined a club in transition; a club that had never really managed to recreate the glory of its past; a club that was still looking to re-establish itself as one of the giants of the European game.

And it was a club that now looked to the past to define its future by bringing in its biggest hero. Kenny Dalglish was appointed Liverpool caretaker manager on 8 January 2011 and, within three weeks, he had brought Suarez in from Amsterdam for a fee of £22.8 million. At the time some within the club baulked at the figure but they would eventually come to realise that the club had nabbed a bargain. Suarez would be worth at least three times that amount within three years. He would become Liverpool's talisman and, arguably, their best buy since Dalglish himself joined the club from Celtic for a fee of £440,000 in 1977. King Kenny had come home to manage the club he lived for and had swiftly brought in the man who would become the new King of the Kop.

The Suarez era at Liverpool had begun.

CHAPTER FOUR

WELCOME TO ANFIELD

After being labelled 'The Cannibal of Ajax' and falling foul of the Dutch FA as his ban for biting PSV Eindhoven's Otman Bakkal was increased to seven league matches, Suarez decided that a move away from Amsterdam would be best for all concerned parties. He felt suffocated in the Dutch Eredivisie; he would admit to friends that it felt claustrophobic and too confined an atmosphere. He needed to break out and express himself in a bigger league; one where he would be just one of several big-name stars, not simply the biggest. So he asked his agent to explore possibilities – to come up with a move that would allow him to move on from his controversies in Holland; a move that would allow him to develop as a player.

Luis wanted to test himself against the best and to be able to prove he could cut it among them; that he could be the best of the best. He also felt victimised that his suspension had been increased and that he would forever be under the spotlight of the Dutch authorities if he did stay in Holland. Luis believed that the two-match suspension agreed with Ajax should have been the end of the matter. The ban meant he would have been out of action until Ajax faced De Graafschap a week into February 2011 – it would have ruled him out of six Eredivisie matches. That was alongside the fine he paid, which he had agreed would go to charity.

He had accepted his punishment via the Ajax two-game ban but was dismayed when he learned he would have to face a much longer spell on the sidelines as the authorities came down much harder on him for his 'act of violence'. For Luis, it was the final straw and would mark the end of his involvement in Dutch football. He knew he had done wrong with the bite but felt the Dutch FA 'were out to get him'; that they would be constantly looking to come down hard on him if he stepped out of line in the future. So he made the irrevocable decision to cut his losses and exit the Netherlands for good.

The majority of Ajax fans were gutted at the news that their hero wanted out. He was a cult hero on the terraces and they knew their team would miss his goals. One fan, calling himself sacredutch, even stepped up to defend Luis over the bite controversy, saying, 'Check out Suarez's personal website where he apologises towards his fans. Suarez is an awesome striker and in the heat of the match and season that he hasn't scored much he gets annoyed and frustrated. The team, fans and himself rely on his goal-scoring skills. How would you feel if you haven't been able to produce at your work over several months, don't you get frustrated?'

But another fan, gig1024, made the point that most Ajax fans agreed with – that Suarez was a genius on the football field but needed to get a grip on his emotions: 'Suarez is great player but he needs to learn to control his temper. He will be no good if he is constantly carded for crazy behavior… and it doesn't get any crazier than biting another [football] player! Come on, Luis, get your head on straight!'

After detailed discussions with Ajax, the club finally accepted the player's wishes to leave and worked in tandem with Suarez's agent Per Guardiola to find a team abroad who would best serve the player's needs – and provide them with the most attractive transfer fee. Initially, Guardiola – the brother of former Barcelona boss Pep – contemplated a move to Spain. But Luis was undecided; if he joined Barca or Real Madrid, he might have to share star billing to the point where he would find himself in and out of the team, such was the star-studded nature of their squads.

No, his dream was to move to a big club but a club that would truly appreciate him and his talents; a club where he was guaranteed a first-team place but where he could develop in tandem with them and where they could share the glory. In short, he wanted to join a football club that had big ambitions and even if they weren't already at the top, they would soon be heading there.

So when Kenny Dalglish came calling, Luis Suarez's dream was answered. In his eyes, Liverpool was the ideal fit at that stage of his career: they were clearly spending big and going places and he could expect to play regularly and, sooner rather than later, win trophies with them. Liverpool were still a legendary name in world football – they had, after all, won the European Cup five times – and were on the brink of reclaiming their place at football's top table after some topsy-turvy years.

Suarez was excited and delighted when Kenny turned up to talk to him. He didn't need to be sold on the club; he knew all about Liverpool and how they had once dominated world club football. And he knew all about – and had total respect for – Dalglish: indeed, Kenny was one of his footballing heroes. Suarez knew he was in the company of one of the greats of world football and was convinced Dalglish was the man he wanted to play for 'within minutes' of their initial get-together.

Kenny told him everything he wanted to hear: that Liverpool were ready to spend big to hit the big-time again and that Luis would have a crucial role to play in the project. And he was honest with him: he admitted that Liverpool were no longer the biggest beasts in the football jungle but he explained slowly and carefully about how he planned to rectify that; how he was going to bring in classy young players who would turn the club around and how he, Luis Suarez, would be the man Dalglish would build his new team around. He told Luis how the owners were 'a hundred per cent behind the project' and how they had given him a transfer chest of upwards of £100 million to get the ship back on course.

Luis asked for a few days to think about it; to talk things over with his agent and his wife Sofia. But he had already made his decision and was just checking that those closest to him were not unduly perturbed by the prospect of him moving to England. So it was no surprise when, at the end of the transfer window in January 2011, Liverpool announced that they had signed Suarez from Ajax for a record fee of €26.5 million (£22.8 million). It was, however, a record that Luis would own only momentarily, for Andy Carroll would soon arrive from Newcastle in an extraordinary £35 million deal.

Yet a year or so before his move to Liverpool, Suarez had expressed his belief that he may not be suited to the hustle-and-bustle football of the Premier League and it was only when he saw how well Carlos Tevez had fared that he changed his mind. He explained his thinking to *The Sunday Times*, saying, 'It's true – I used to think that English football was not my style. But I saw Carlos Tevez play at Boca and Corinthians and I never imagined that he would play in the Premier League.

'When I see the way that Tevez plays there I think I can be a big name in England. It's because of the energy, and the spirit they put into the game in England. Now, I think it's a kind of football that suits me.'

The news of his imminent departure to Merseyside was soon out on the streets of Amsterdam and Ajax fans groaned at the realisation that their star man and goal king was on his way. They gave him a hero's send-off after their 1–0 win over Venlose Voetbal Vereniging in the Eredivisie. He was still suspended but was clearly moved by the tributes of the Ajax management and the loyal supporters, who clapped their hands in tribute as the departing hero walked around the pitch for the final time as an Ajax player.

Ajax assistant manager, Danny Blind, spoke through a microphone on the pitch to thank Suarez for his three-and-a-half-year spell at the club. Blind said, 'You came to us as a young player with long hair. But you grew with us. You became a top scorer, captain and father. It's time for a new step, although we regret to see you go. We would have loved to keep you with us for longer.

'You were the tops for us in pretty much every category in that time: most attempts on goal, most goals scored, most assists and also most hits on the crossbar or the post. But one statistic says it all: a hundred and eleven goals for Ajax in a hundred and fifty-nine games.'

The applause echoed around the ground as the Ajax fans nodded their heads in agreement: here was a man who had served them well and deserved their best wishes, even if he was deserting them for pastures new. After Blind's speech, Suarez kicked fifty balls into the stands and then thanked the club and the fans for their kindness and generosity of spirit.

His final words were, 'Thank you for everything and see you later!'

He would later admit that he owed a great debt to Ajax and Dutch football for helping him develop as a player and a person, saying,

Even as a kid in Uruguay, I knew I would one day have to play in Europe. And I saw Holland as a great school. I learned so much in my time in Holland and, because of the way they do things there, I don't think I would have learned as much somewhere else. I was a selfish player. But they taught me the importance of being part of a team. Van Basten taught me a lot about how to play as a forward; about shooting techniques and about things that worked for him. His movement, his technique.

But from all of them I learned about remaining calm on the pitch; when in front of goal and also when being fouled. You have to try not to react; take a step back. I learned to control my attitude more.

So he did have a tear in his eye as he left the Ajax Arena pitch for the last time, the words of Danny Blind and the applause and appreciation of the fans still ringing in his ears. Then he gave a final wave to the adoring legions and he was on his way: to England, to Liverpool. To Kenny Dalglish and a new venture, a new project and a new aim – to put Liverpool right back at the top of British and world football with goals galore.

The clubs now put out official statements to confirm the deal. Ajax said,

Ajax and Liverpool have reached an agreement regarding the transfer of Luis Suarez. The transfer to the English club is effective immediately. The relocation involves a total sum of up to €26.5 million. The Uruguayan international was under contract with Ajax until June 30, 2013. Suarez was born on January 24, 1987 in Salto, Uruguay. He came to Ajax from FC Groningen in 2007, having previously played for Nacional. He made his debut in Amsterdam on August 15, 2007, in the Ajax-Slavia Prague match (0–1). The forward played a total of 159 official matches for Ajax, scoring 111 goals. He was the Eredivisie's top scorer last season with 35 goals.

And a statement on Liverpool's official website declared, 'Liverpool football club announced this afternoon that they had agreed a fee of up to €26.5 million with Ajax for the transfer of Luis Suarez, subject to the completion of a medical. The club have now been given permission by Ajax to discuss personal terms with the player and his representatives.'

There had been a slight hold-up in the deal when Ajax coach Frank de Boer apparently told his board that he would rather keep the player than accept the suggested fee; that he believed (and quite rightly as it turned out) that Luis was worth far more than £22 million. De Boer had bristled at the very beginning of negotiations when Liverpool had initially offered a figure just less than £13 million. He had told them to come back with a 'respectful' bid and a club official backed the stance, saying,

> We'll have to wait for them to come back with something more respectful. We want to keep him – at least until the end of the season and preferably for the rest of his contract. If you compare the €15 million [£12.7 million] Liverpool want to pay for Suarez with other transfers, you can imagine that it's far too low for us. Luis is our top goal-scorer for the last three years and also the man with by far the most assists as well.
>
> He was one of the big guys for Uruguay in helping them come third in the World Cup in the summer and he still has a contract with us for two and a half years.

De Boer was still not completely happy with the final amount his board had accepted, even though it meant Ajax would make a £16.3 million profit on the fee they had paid Groningen in 2007.

De Boer's belief was that, if Ajax kept Suarez another year, they could easily earn another £10 million on top of the £22 million figure. But it was too late: Luis's mind was made up and De Boer and Ajax reluctantly accepted his wishes. It was their parting thank you to him, for all the goals he had scored for them in his time at the club.

De Boer had slowly realised that he would not be able to keep the striker and had put in place plans for a replacement. He had told the Dutch press early in January 2011, 'I've had a showdown with Luis. I wanted to know what his plans are and what the future will bring. Luis is training hard. He told me that if a big club comes in for him now he is ready to talk to them. I've a back-up scenario ready.'

Then, when Liverpool made that first offer, he added, 'I can understand Luis wanting to go to Liverpool. It's a beautiful club but then it has to be satisfying for both parties.'

Of course, with the benefit of hindsight, it is easy to see how very correct De Boer was about Luis's valuation being too low, especially when you consider that Liverpool would splash out £35 million on the relatively unproven Carroll just hours after tying up the deal for Suarez. But Dalglish was not complaining; he was delighted and with good reason. He had secured the services of the man he believed would now score the goals that would take Liverpool onwards and upwards. For many months he had had his eye on Suarez and, if anyone could be guaranteed to sign a man who would definitely deliver goals, it was surely Dalglish, one of the greatest goal-scorers EVER.

It was revealed that Suarez, twenty-four, would wear the coveted number-seven shirt made famous by Dalglish – and that he himself had asked for it. He knew all about the exploits of Dalglish and other Kop legends such as Kevin Keegan and it was a sign of his confidence that he felt able to pull on the famous shirt and continue the tradition of excellence it embellished.

The Uruguayan, who scored 49 goals in 48 games in the Eredivisie in his last season at Ajax, said,

It's a dream to be able to come and play here. Liverpool is a very famous club, the most famous club in England, and I watched Liverpool and English football as a boy. My aim is to work, to show the fans how hard I am ready to work. I want to put in lots of effort, to show people my capabilities.

First of all I want to try to play as many games as possible and help move us up the table. My ambitions for the future are to do my very best for Liverpool, to try to learn more about English football and to become a champion.

At another press conference in his early days at Liverpool, he would then add,

I know there are people who doubt I can be a success in one of the top leagues but this is an opportunity for me to show what I can do at one of the very biggest clubs in the world. My aim is to score at the same rate as I did with Ajax but maybe that will not be so easy in this tough Premier League.

This is the right moment in my career to play at the next level. My time at Ajax was perfect in so many ways and I will always owe the club so much for giving me a chance to move my game forward but Liverpool is something special. To score in front of the famous Kop and to be given the number-seven shirt so many legends have worn is incredible for me.

As well as being King Kenny's first signing on his return to the club as manager, Luis was also the first major signing for Liverpool owners New England Sports Ventures (NESV) since it bought the club in October 2010. It would also turn out to be the best signing for both Kenny and NESV. Dalglish would go on to be criticised during his reign for some of the signings he made, with many accusing him of wasting money on the likes of Carroll and Charlie Adam, but no one could argue over the merits of Suarez. It was a pure-genius purchase and one he deserves full credit, even years later.

Naturally, he was delighted with his new signing and looked like the proverbial cat that had got the cream when he paraded him at a press conference. Kenny said,

We're delighted to get Luis. He's got a fantastic goal-scoring record. He's scored goals for Ajax and at the World Cup and is somebody I think will really excite the fans. I think great credit must go to the new owners. They have really put their stamp down. They promised money would be made available during the transfer window; one or two sceptics doubted that but they are not doubting now! The ambition is there for everyone to see. When we said there was money available, we said we would do our best to spend it responsibly, and [Suarez] is a signing which reflects this.

The owners have been as good as gold. They have stuck to their word and they have shown great determination to move the club forward. This is a great reward for the supporters and players, who have been fantastic since I came in three or four weeks ago. All round, it is a fantastic day for the football club.

Asked what Suarez's main attributes were, he replied simply, 'Luis scores goals. He is quick, intelligent and has had a fantastic education at Ajax. We are looking forward to working with him and, fingers crossed, everyone will be happy with his signing. Often people come across to the Premier League and fail, not just from Holland. But why focus on the negativity? We would not bring him in unless we felt he could adapt. This is a positive move for the club and we should enjoy it, instead of focusing on the negativity.'

And what did Kenny make of Luis taking his special number-seven shirt? 'I never made the number-seven shirt famous – Kevin [Keegan] did. I was just fortunate enough to come to a fantastic club after Kevin and my number happened to be seven. We don't want Luis to be like myself or like Kevin, we want him to be himself and to come and play. There will be no pressure on him, we just want him to give his best. There is certainly no comparison to be made. He is certainly a better player than Kevin and myself are now, so he hasn't got much to beat!'

A few days later, Dalglish would still be purring when asked how Luis was settling in. He beamed a big smile and said, 'He has not even had the opportunity to train with us because of administrative stuff which had to be sorted out. When he starts training with the lads, I think we might see an improvement. He has a big smile on his face every day. He's happy and a good guy.'

At the same time, Luis was asked how he believed things were going and he, too, smiled but with a steely determination showed that he meant business; that he planned to be a big success at Anfield: 'This is the biggest chance to show what I can do at a major club and I will not let it pass by me,' he said. 'My life when I was growing up was never easy and I appreciate everything that is happening for me now. Football has given so much to my whole family and I will not take anything for granted now that I have arrived at Liverpool.'

Liverpool fans certainly laid out the welcome mat for the little Uruguayan when he arrived at Anfield. Hundreds turned out to greet him and he happily signed autographs. And the general feeling among the fans was that the club had got a £23 million bargain, given his goal-scoring exploits in Holland. One Koppite said, 'I actually think he's a pretty good deal at 23 mil. Players from less-reputed leagues are often derided because "It's harder to score goals in the Premier League" –

but the simple fact that teams in the PL usually have better-quality defenders means jack-all because of a certain gung-ho, attacking element still very much present. We've seen this before with van Nistelrooy or Roy Makaay (though admittedly not so much with Huntelaar), so I'd say, if you have that impressive a scoring record in the Eredivisie, chances are you will come up with the goods at a higher level.'

And the Liverpool players were certainly delighted with the signing of Suarez. They believed that the deal to snap up one of Europe's most prolific goal-scorers showed the club now meant business and defender Jamie Carragher called on the board to now turn Dalglish's caretaker role into a full-time one as recognition for the work he had done since taking over from the grey days of Roy Hodgson. Carragher said,

I have great respect for Roy, so I'd never say 'things have changed for the better' and that type of stuff. As a club and as players we didn't do enough to help the manager out – the performances weren't good enough and obviously the managers take the brunt of it. But things have improved now and Kenny coming has got everyone onside. It's not our decision if he gets the job. That's up to the club owners. But for everyone, especially me and Stevie [Gerrard], he's a hero to us. The results are obviously going very well. If you're asking me, obviously I'd love him to be the manager.

Many Liverpool fans also felt that Suarez, with his fluent Spanish, would prove an ideal foil up front for Fernando

Torres, who seemed to have lost some of his power in previous weeks. One supporter, Patrick, summed up that belief, saying, 'Goals are what we need. Our defence will be fine as soon as we have Carra and Agger back together. We could use a true left-back but it can wait. Kelly on the right, Johnson on the left is not ideal but not the crisis that it has been made out to be. The absence of SG and Carra cannot be overstated but will be fixed soon.

'Suarez up with Torres does allow SG to play as an attacking midfielder or a holding midfielder. This plays to SG's strength, which is a box-to-box midi. Raul can hold behind him and Kuyt can have the length of right side of the field.'

The only problem with Patrick's theory was that it would remain just that: a theory. For, not long after Suarez put pen to paper at Anfield, Torres was doing just the same away from Anfield... at Stamford Bridge. Just as Suarez was signing on the dotted line, so twenty-six-year-old Torres was handing in a written transfer request. Initially, it was rejected by the club. A statement on the official Liverpool website read, 'Fernando Torres tonight submitted a written transfer request, which has been rejected by Liverpool. Fernando is under a long-term contract and the club expects him to honour the commitment he made to Liverpool FC and its supporters when he signed the agreement.'

Liverpool still had hopes that Torres would stay if he saw they were splashing out on top-class players like Suarez. They further stressed their intention to keep the big Spaniard by adding that he was 'not for sale'. But it would all be to no avail – Torres had made his mind up and even the signing of

Luis was not enough to persuade him to do a U-turn. Two days after saying he would never leave, Torres did just that. Chelsea had upped their bid from £35 million to £50 million – a British record transfer deal. Torres signed a five-and-a-half-year contract at Stamford Bridge, which would keep him at the club until 2016. The deal was confirmed minutes after the close of the January transfer window.

Speaking to Chelsea's official website after completing his move, Torres said, 'I am very happy with my transfer to Chelsea and I am looking forward very much to helping my new team-mates this season and for many years to come. Having played against Chelsea many times since coming to England, and in some very big games I will never forget, I know there are many great players here and I will work hard to win a place in the team. I hope I can score some important goals for the supporters to enjoy this season.'

Chelsea's chairman Bruce Buck added, 'This is a very significant day for Chelsea, capturing one of the best players in the world with his peak years ahead of him. We have long admired the talents of a player who is a proven goal-scorer in English football and Fernando's arrival is a sign of our continuing high ambitious. I hope every Chelsea fan is as excited as I am with this news.'

The big Spanish hitman had decided his future would be best served at Chelsea, so the Kop would never get the chance to see how the Torres/Suarez axis might have worked out. Liverpool fans were, naturally, despondent and angered by Torres's decision to abandon them: he was dubbed a 'Judas' and 'a traitor' on fan sites, although he himself felt strongly enough about the accusations to issue a statement of his own. In it, he said,

> I think 'traitor' makes no sense. I played three very good seasons there, left massive money there, lots of goals, good performances. I'm very happy with everything I did there.
>
> I never kissed the Liverpool badge. Never. No. Kissed the badge? No. I never did. I never did when I was at Atletico Madrid and I love Atletico, my former club. I see some players doing that when they join a club but the romance in football has gone. It's a different thing now. People are coming and leaving. When you are joining a club you want to do the best for yourself and that club and that's all.
>
> Some people like to kiss the badge. They can do it. I only want to score goals and do my job and achieve all the targets the team has. When I was born in Madrid I was not a Liverpool fan or a Chelsea fan. I was only an Atletico Madrid fan. I still am. Maybe it's the only badge I will kiss if I have to kiss one.

Torres's controversial exit would mean a new striker coming in to partner Suarez, as Newcastle's number nine, Andy Carroll, arrived at Anfield in a £35 million deal. Both moves were bone shakers – who would have thought Torres would leave what he had said was 'his beloved Anfield' and the fans who had worshipped him, and who would have thought Carroll was worth £35 million when his career was still in its infancy?

Torres joined Chelsea on the final day of the winter transfer window, just two days after Suarez passed a medical to complete his move to Anfield. It was a shock to Suarez, who had fully expected to be playing alongside Torres in what, on paper at least, looked a formidable attack. Suarez would later admit as much, saying, 'Yes, it's true I expected to play with Fernando. Fernando is a very good player. He's got great quality and it would have been nice to play with him. It's a shame that he's gone as he is an excellent player and has great qualities but at the same time there are many other great players at Liverpool. When one top player goes, perhaps another great player comes in.'

Luis went on to tell Goal.com UK that he simply got down to business and worked on developing a different partnership with Carroll:

He and Torres are very different players. Andy has had an injury and he's just starting to come back into the game. They have different qualities and ways of playing the game, so you can't really make comparisons. They have different styles – one might be better at one thing and the other better at something else. Andy is a big, strong player with many qualities and it will be exciting to play with him. And having a manager like Kenny Dalglish is really great for me. He is a person of great history and importance at the club. He's one of the best players the club has ever had and now he's correcting me and training me.

Suarez may have been disappointed that he would not, after all, be lining up with Torres but he relished the opportunity of a partnership with Carroll who, with his massive physique and strength, would surely prove a marvellous bulwark for him; someone who would surely create the space in which he would thrive. Dalglish had pulled off one coup with the signing of Suarez but had he worked a similar stroke of genius not long after by flogging Torres and bringing in Andy Carroll to partner the brilliant Uruguayan?

CHAPTER FIVE

CANNY KENNY

The first inkling that there might be a deal to bring Andy Carroll to Liverpool to link up with Luis came around lunchtime on transfer-deadline day. The Press Association filed a snap announcing that a £25 million bid for Carroll had been dismissed by Newcastle. A couple of hours later it leaked out that the bid had risen to £30 million but that Newcastle had still turned it down.

Amid the sports desks of Fleet Street the discussions centred upon two factors – Liverpool must have already accepted that Torres was on his way to Chelsea (subject to passing a medical) and that they were now clearly intent on making Carroll the man to replace him in the number-nine shirt. The next discussion was based around conjecture – surely Mike Ashley, the man who owned Newcastle United, would sell Carroll if, say, the Kop kings increased their offer by another £5 million.

There was widespread surprise that he had not accepted the £30 million – after all, he was a businessman and, from a purely business point of view, the sale of a homegrown asset for a £30 million profit presented sound sense.

Ashley had been trying to sell the club over the previous two years, so surely taking £30 million profit on one deal would have tempted him.

The feeling within the Street was that, yes, he was interested in even £25 million or £30 million but that his gut instinct told him there was more money to be made. Liverpool were clearly desperate to land their man. Like Newcastle, they would be selling their star asset but, unlike the Toon, they were keen to immediately reinvest a large chunk of that into bringing in a new player who could ease the pain of their genius's departure.

By 4.33pm on 31 January, I had been told by a friend connected with Liverpool FC that a deal had been agreed to buy Carroll for £35.5 million, subject to him agreeing personal terms and passing a medical. I emailed another football-writer friend on another national newspaper with the bombshell news and asked him if he thought Andy would do well on Merseyside, what he reckoned to the deal and whether he would become an immediate idol.

He replied, 'If he scores a few and gets in the England team may be OK. World's gone mad!'

Short and to the point; but had the world gone mad? Or, more precisely, had Liverpool FC gone mad? I don't agree that they had. They had secured the services of the man whom, according to ITV pundit and former player Andy Townsend, was 'a special, special player – someone who would lead the England attack for many, many years to come'.

They had been forced to pay £35 million but they had a sackful of cash in the bank after the Torres sale went through. The departure of Torres gave them Andy Carroll and an extra £15 million in the bank. Not a bad deal when you think they were getting a man who would give every ounce of sweat and blood for the cause – and they were also unloading a man who had given nothing remotely like that commitment for some time.

Not a bad deal when you also consider that most people in football believed Carroll was worth upwards of at least £25 million at the time the transfer-deadline window finally closed that stunning January day. A day earlier I was told that Tottenham had made an opening bid of £23 million for Carroll but had been knocked back by the Toon. Indeed, Spurs manager Harry Redknapp – while denying he had been involved in negotiations – did admit that his chairman, Daniel Levy, may have been involved in negotiations for Andy. Redknapp said, 'I never made a bid for Andy Carroll. Maybe the chairman did but I never did.'

The *Sunday Sun* newspaper, covering the northeast, confirmed that story on 30 January, saying,

Newcastle United have rejected another massive bid for Andy Carroll from Spurs – and told Harry Redknapp not to bother coming back with a fresh offer tomorrow. Tottenham chairman Daniel Levy spoke directly to Mike Ashley on Friday night and offered £23 million for the

England striker, but Newcastle rebuffed an offer they believe is derisory for a player of his potential.

Sources in North London have suggested Spurs will be back for the player in the next 24 hours with an improved offer which would include loaning a striker to St James' Park.

But even though Newcastle have enquired about Roman Pavlyuchenko, Peter Crouch and Robbie Keane during January, they will not be budged on Carroll – who is rated at more than £30 million by the club. United's resolve is impressive and it will be welcomed on Tyneside...

The last sentence would prove rather ironic given that twenty-four hours later Carroll was gone but it was clear right up to the sale that Ashley wanted top dollar for his top player. It was also clear that Newcastle were tempted even by the early morning offer of £30 million for Carroll – otherwise why did they delay (in the late morning) and then cancel (at lunchtime) the planned afternoon press conference by Pardew?

Clearly a deal was in the air. It was just the final fee that needed establishing. By late afternoon Carroll was on his way to Liverpool after the club had accepted the new £35.5 million bid. He took a private helicopter trip so that he would be at Liverpool's Melwood training ground for an evening medical.

Initially, the medical had been planned for 5pm but that, too, was delayed as the two clubs thrashed out the final details of the biggest transfer deal involving a British player. Finally, both clubs issued statements on their official websites confirming the shock news that the deal had been agreed in principle.

Newcastle said, 'A transfer request has been agreed between Newcastle United and Liverpool for Magpies striker Andy Carroll. The 22-year-old England international has this afternoon handed in a transfer request, which has reluctantly been accepted by the club, and Carroll is currently in talks with The Reds over a move to Anfield.'

Liverpool said, 'Liverpool FC confirmed this afternoon that Newcastle United had accepted a club record offer for the transfer of Andy Carroll. The club have been given permission by Newcastle to discuss personal terms with the player, who will now travel to Liverpool for a medical.'

Chelsea had still not confirmed that Liverpool had accepted their bid for Torres but by 6pm it was apparent that the deal that would fund the Carroll transfer was also now in full motion as the Spaniard headed down from the northwest to Stamford Bridge for his medical. I am told that he had not yet agreed personal terms but that his salary was never going to be a problem, so keen was he to join the Blues.

So Carroll travelled down by helicopter and put in a transfer request to get out of Toon. That makes it seem like he was keen to quit his boyhood club but I am told that wasn't the case; that he loves Newcastle United FC and always will and that he did ask to stay; that he asked for a new deal that would show how much the club valued his services. Pardew would later agree that Carroll had asked for a new deal and that he was told there would be none and that he needed to put in a transfer request if he wanted to see what was on offer at Liverpool.

It also emerged that Newcastle would help him get to Liverpool by allowing him to make use of said private helicopter (which belonged to Mike Ashley).

Do all those comments add up to a man wanting to get out of Toon as quickly as possible – or do they add up to the bosses at Newcastle wanting to get him out so that they could bank the £35.5 million his sale would bring?

The *Sun* had no doubt that it was a case of the latter. Shaun Custis wrote,

> Newcastle were so desperate to get rid of Andy Carroll they laid on chairman Mike Ashley's private helicopter to fly him to Liverpool.
>
> But Carroll insisted he could have been talked into staying at St James' Park for less than the Kop offered if Newcastle had bothered to try. And he claimed Toon managing director Derek Llambias told him the club was desperate to cash in on their prize asset.
>
> Carroll said, 'I didn't want to leave at all. Derek Llambias asked me to hand in a transfer request, so I was pushed into a corner. I wasn't wanted by them and they made it clear they wanted the money. Then I flew down in the helicopter. I'm gutted that I wasn't wanted at my home team after everything I have done.

Carroll had signed a new £20,000 a week, five-year contract at Newcastle in October 2010. The five-and-a-half-year deal he signed with Liverpool would see his salary increase to £80,000 a week for the first year, with further incremental rises built in.

Not surprisingly, Pardew and Llambias disputed Andy's version of events, claiming they did not want him to leave. Llambias said,

We didn't push Andy Carroll out, far from it – he asked to go. The fact is Mike Ashley didn't want to sell him, it's not like he needs the money, is it? And remember, we turned down bids of £30 million and then £35 million from Liverpool.

That's serious money for a twenty-two-year-old with only six months' experience in the Premier League. But finally Mike's point of view was the player's put in a transfer request, so what can we do? Andy was already earning top money at the club after signing a new deal recently... But he said he'd been offered £80,000 a week from Liverpool and asked what we would pay to make him stay. We told him the club just couldn't afford to give him a deal like that, nothing close. And when we said 'No' – well, that's when he put in his transfer request... Yes, he went in our helicopter. But the sooner the deal was done, the sooner we could make our own moves in the transfer market. It was already very late. We will spend in the summer. Every penny of the £35 million will stay in the club.

The latter part of that argument did rather fall flat, as Newcastle bought absolutely no one that day after the Carroll deal went through – even though Ashley's copter got him there in double-quick time.

But Toon manager Pardew added, 'If he had really wanted to stay, he could have. We certainly didn't twist his arm to put in the transfer request or get on the helicopter. He had a five-year contract, a contract we said we would renew in the summer, but he wanted to renew it straight away.'

Simon Bird, writing in the *Daily Mirror*, was fierce in his condemnation of Pardew and Newcastle, saying,

Alan Pardew can't play a cheque for £35 million up front. Newcastle United can't cheer and celebrate because the club's bank balance suddenly looks very healthy. Pardew is understood to be furious that Carroll has been sold. Understandably. Not a quitting moment, but certainly unhappy. He put his credibility and power as the newly installed boss at St James' Park on the line in making those declarations.

Newcastle is now a selling club, like they were in the 1980s when Peter Beardsley, Paul Gascoigne and Chris Waddle were peddled to the highest bidders rather than forming the nucleus of a team.

Writing in the *Daily Mail*, Martin Samuel suggested that the blame for the exit lay with both sides but that they were both fearful of saying so because of the reaction it might cause with the Toon fans. Samuel said,

If we were more grown-up about this all sides could tell the truth. Carroll could acknowledge that, as much as he loved his hometown club, the salary and opportunity to play for Liverpool under Kenny Dalglish was too good to resist; the owners of Newcastle could say the same of a £35 million transfer fee for a player who has experienced one half of a good season in the Premier League.

Sadly, football is no longer a reasonable place. Any player that leaves is a traitor, no matter what the circumstances, and any board that sells should be sacked, no matter the worth of the transaction to the business.

It was an interesting angle. Certainly, the Newcastle fans were split over whether the player or the management was to blame for his departure. One fan summed up the general feeling of dismay felt in Tyneside when he said, 'Pardew, if you have any man parts, you will resign. Other clubs would then value your integrity and you may get another chance. But look at the mess you are in now. You are Ashley's puppet. Does he tell you who to play too?'

Some others felt the club had no choice but to cash in. Another fan said, 'I am upset he has gone but the FACT is he signed a five-year contact with Newcastle just in October – but when he saw the interest from a couple of other clubs, he wanted and asked for a new contact (give me a break).

'What is even more surprising is Pardew told Carroll they would give him a new contract in the summer but Carroll wanted it right away. I know the fans' reaction right now is to blame the club but, when they hear all of the facts, I think they will change their opinion.'

As if to rub salt into the wound, Newcastle fans who opened their club calendar on the day after their hero had gone were sickened to find Andy smiling back at them! Yes, irony of ironies, he was the face of February – the pin-up for the whole month. Charity-shop assistant manager Maria Keane, forty-nine, who bought the calendar for her son Sean, sixteen, told the *Daily Star*, 'It's an astonishing coincidence. No one could have imagined his picture would last longer at United than him.'

But there was no divergence of opinion about Andy Carroll at Liverpool FC at the time of his signing. He may have cost a fortune, he may have been overpriced by up to £10 million in some of their eyes, but what the hell – the club could afford it. Yes, there were only a very few dissenters at the signing who had put a real smile back on their faces. To prove it, Carroll's car was mobbed by Liverpool fans when he arrived for his medical at Melwood and the feeling was that King Kenny had bought a player who would bring back the good times to the club, who would prove he was worth every penny of his transfer fee and who would eventually be worth much more.

One Liverpool fan said, 'Welcome to Anfield, Andy Carroll, you will enjoy playing here. We lost the sulk but now we got a number-nine HULK. You look to be a better TEAM player than the number nine who lied to us and left. You will outdo him, I'm sure of that. I hope you beat his record of quickest goals.'

And another added, 'This is a lad with a big bright future and if we didn't buy him now then in a year or two he will be worth twice as much. Andy, come and enjoy the club and the fans and you will get everything Torres has lost. Can't wait to see you in a red shirt.'

Dalglish was just as delighted as the fans that he had got his man. He said he had been eyeing Carroll as the ideal centre-forward to work off Suarez in what could be a productive 'Little & Large' combo and that the duel signings proved just how big a draw Liverpool FC remained in the modern game. He followed it up by saying,

Suarez could have gone to other clubs, he had choices of a few places, but he wanted to come here. I think that's really important.

It's encouraging that there are still massive players out there who want to play for the club and have a feeling for the club... The owners have been as good as gold. They have stuck to their word, and they have shown great determination to move the club forward. All round, it is a fantastic day for the football club. While we have a realisation we cannot hold onto the past, the history and tradition of the football club, neither can it be used as a noose around our neck. That should be a great signal for everybody to drive forward and make their own history.

Suarez also admitted he was looking forward to working with Carroll and that he was confident they would strike up a fine partnership at Anfield. He revealed that he, like Dalglish, believed that the signings confirmed Liverpool remained at the forefront of European club football and that they could now go on to achieve further honours. He said, 'Liverpool is a very famous club, the most famous club in England, and I watched

Liverpool and English football as a boy. It's a dream to be able to come and play here, it is that simple.'

Dalglish had spoken with admiration for the club's new American owner, John W. Henry, and the man himself explained that the only condition of the Carroll purchase he had set himself was that Liverpool ended up with £15 million in cash after the sale of Torres.

'The fee for Torres was dependent on what Newcastle asked for Carroll,' Henry told the *Guardian*. 'The negotiation for us was simply the difference in prices paid by Chelsea and to Newcastle. Those prices could have been £35 million [from Chelsea for Torres] and £20 million [to Newcastle for Carroll], 40 and 25 or 50 and 35. It was ultimately up to Newcastle how much this was all going to cost. They [Newcastle] made a hell of a deal. We felt the same way.'

The views of those within the game – other managers and players – gradually also started to filter in. Perhaps unsurprisingly, Harry Redknapp was quick to say Carroll had been 'too dear' – unsurprising in the sense that he had lost out on the player after his £23 million bid was rejected by Newcastle. Redknapp said, 'Carroll was too dear; he's a real prospect and could turn out to be a bargain. No one knows how he's going to do at Liverpool but he's certainly got the potential to be a top player. It would have been a big gamble. It could come off but it wasn't one that we were prepared to take.'

Similarly, Gary McAllister, the former Scotland player and now number two to Gerard Houllier at Aston Villa, reckoned that Liverpool had got it wrong. He argued that they should have done a deal for Carroll at the start of the transfer window to get him more cheaply and that Darren Bent, who had joined Villa from Sunderland for £24 million earlier in the window, was a much better buy. McAllister said,

We did our business nice and early in the window and, when you see the prices at the back end of the transfer window, it looks like we've got ourselves a bargain. Is he better value for money than Torres and Carroll? Yes, I would say he is. Outstanding value.

Maybe five or six years ago you would have called us all crazy if we were throwing these numbers about – but that is the going rate and market forces dictate the price. Darren is proven in the Premier League. He has been in and around it a long time and he is a natural goal-scorer.

You go back to Shearer and Owen and Lineker and I don't think you can coach that goal-scoring art into someone. It is a natural instinct, knowing where to go and arriving at the right time. Darren has lifted the place since he came in, there's no doubt about that.

Former Newcastle hero Tino Asprilla said he thought his old club had got the better end of the deal: 'Was Andy worth £35 million? Maybe no. Newcastle were very lucky to get that deal. It's a great deal for them. He was a great player for them but maybe Newcastle can buy three or even four Andy Carrolls.'

But the Colombian maybe had an axe to grind with Dalglish from the time he played under him at Newcastle. Asprilla added, 'I would say to Andy, make sure he scores goals or he will get dropped straight away. He will also need a translator to understand Dalglish's Scottish accent! I couldn't understand a word he said. One day he spent half an hour on a drawing board telling me how I should play. Then he asked me after thirty minutes and asked me if I understood. I had to turn round and say, "I don't have a clue." Kenny said he'd explain another time but we never had that conversation.'

Another former Toon star, Andy Cole, also questioned the Carroll deal while applauding Chelsea's purchase of Torres: 'I actually believe that Chelsea got a bargain with Torres,' he told Goal.com. 'OK, £50 million is a lot of money, but that's what you pay for a top-class striker – and the guy is world class.

'As for Carroll, that is a big gamble by Liverpool. He was doing well for Newcastle, but £35 million is a heck of a lot to spend on a player with limited experience. That surprised me, I have to say. Liverpool had taken a big chance on this guy and we'll wait to see whether it pays off or not. If it does, what a move, but that is no guarantee.'

Cole himself was once the subject of similar debate on Tyneside and around the country. In 1995 then Newcastle manager Kevin Keegan controversially decided to sell the striker to arch rivals Manchester United for £7 million. And Steve Howey, who was part of the team at St James' that Cole left behind, contends that the departure of Cole was a much bigger shock than Carroll's leaving. He said,

I was shocked that Andy Carroll went when he did but not really surprised. I think selling Andy [Cole] was worse. Manchester United were a major rival to us and we were both vying for the title and there was a big worry that it would come back to haunt us. The difference with Andy Carroll is that he's a local lad, he's been given the number-nine shirt and a new long-term contract.

It seemed like both parties wanted him to stay – but then a big offer like that comes in and everything changes. But it isn't in the same league as when Cole went, for me.

Another former Toon star, Alan Shearer, now a *Match of the Day* pundit, added that he believed Carroll would do well under the guidance of former master striker Dalglish: 'He's going to a club that has to win trophies, is expected to win trophies. He's going there with a great manager who I'm sure will get the very best out of him.'

Former Toon chairman Freddy Shepherd also insisted on having his say, claiming Ashley should have refused to sell. Shepherd said, 'I signed Andy as a lad and it's a sad day for Newcastle. When I was chairman Liverpool tried to buy Alan Shearer and I refused point blank. It can be done. If Newcastle don't need the money then why sell him? A few weeks ago he signed a new contract and said he wanted to stay with the club forever. They should have said that as he's just signed a new deal he isn't going. Having said that, good luck to Liverpool. They've done a great deal. Andy Carroll will be England's centre-forward for the next ten years.'

So what did Big Andy Carroll, the man at the centre of the storm, have to say on the transfer that had left us all stunned? Well, in his first press conference as a Liverpool player, Andy said he would prove he was a more mature character than many of the daily papers had painted him, that he would give everything for Liverpool, that he would handle the spotlight placed on him – but that he would still enjoy 'his pint'. Carroll said,

> I don't mind a pint now and again but that is the way I have been brought up. That's who I am and I am not really going to change. I am just going to carry on playing my football, keep my head down and do it at the right time. I have made some mistakes in the past but they are all behind me. I just have to move on into the future.
>
> I am aware the spotlight is on me. I know they will be watching what I'm doing. I have to deal with it and take it in my stride. It has been a massive change in the last year or so… getting promoted, getting the number-nine shirt, getting in the England squad and then coming to one of the world's greatest clubs. It's very different to playing in the Championship. It has been so fast and, thinking about it now, it does seem a very big change.

Carroll added that he was already a confident person – pointing to his demanding the famed number-nine shirt as proof of that. He said,

> I knew it was empty and knew I'd done well the season before in the Championship, so I went into the office and asked for it. Watching Shearer when I had a season ticket, that was the shirt I wanted when I was growing

up. I know I can play, I know I can score goals, so I can handle the spotlight.

It's a great chance for me to come to a club like Liverpool and show what I can do. I've been at Newcastle all my life and I've shown what I can do there, but stepping away from where I've been brought up and know everyone, it's a big change. It's a great deal of money, but I'm sure I can prove it here as well.

Kenny Dalglish was just as confident that his new boy would show he was the business and that he would soon become the latest Kop idol. Dalglish, who was born in Glasgow and played for Celtic and who played and managed Liverpool and managed Newcastle, said, 'Glasgow, Newcastle and Liverpool are similar. The history of the places, the shipyards, the people, the fanaticism towards their clubs; but Newcastle is a bit different because there is only one club in the city.

'Apart from his abilities as a footballer, what will be endearing to our supporters will be his innocence, his youth.'

Kenny was annoyed by the way many pundits had questioned his judgement in spending £35 million on Carroll as a partner for Luis Suarez up front. Dalglish said,

I don't want it to be negative in any way, shape or form about Andy Carroll signing for Liverpool football club. He's a great signing for us, as is Luis' signing, it's fantastic for us. And we can reassure Andy that we're more positive than yourselves are [the media]. We're really looking forward to getting him up and ready and working and I'm sure he's anxious as well but he's just got to be conscious of the fact that he doesn't push too hard. So we'll look after him, get him fit and he'll play when he's fit and ready. It might be a few weeks but we never signed him for a few weeks, we signed him for five and a half years. So that's what we're looking forward to.

Dalglish then made a point of saying that Carroll was his number-one choice for the number-nine shirt. He said,

He's got fantastic potential. He's already part of the England squad and for us it's a fantastic signing... He's the best person we could have got in here to wear the number-nine shirt and at such a young age, when you consider that he wore the number-nine at Newcastle, which is a fantastic honour, and he can wear the number-nine here as well.

For somebody at twenty-two years of age that's a lot to carry on your shoulders and he's showed by what he did at Newcastle that he's capable of doing that. Anybody that can wear that number-nine shirt up there and score goals has got a chance. We know that he's only a young boy. We know the price might be a bit more than what some people think it should be – but then every single person in here has got to justify their wages and their costs so if you can do that with yourselves then surely he can do that for us.

It was an impassioned plea for patience and for the boy to be given a fair chance. And it was typical Dalglish; throwing himself in front of the headlights to shield his new boy. It was Dalglish the master manager in full flow and Dalglish the decent, admirable human being in full flow. Always a great, loyal servant to Liverpool football club, he was now just as determined that the boy he had chosen for stardom at Anfield would be shielded and protected from the hungry pack of press wolves queuing up for a piece of the action at the Shankly Gates.

However, an icon of the modern game – and one of the finest strikers in the world – expressed the opinion that Carroll and Suarez would form a lethal partnership. Spain's David Villa, the man who scored the winner in the World Cup final in 2010, said, 'Each year there are big transfers of this type. It's normal. All teams need to strengthen when they want to win things. Liverpool needed to reinforce after the sale of Fernando [Torres]. Carroll and Suarez are two great players who are worth every penny. I'm sure they'll be a hit with the fans.'

Carroll had arrived and was eager to link up with Luis Suarez to form that lethal partnership. And the last word as he settled into Anfield came from his new partner in crime. Suarez said, 'I am aware of Andy's style. I've seen quite a bit of him playing for Newcastle on television in Holland. He looks the typical number nine and the type who suits my game perfectly.'

The Dalglish dream team in attack was in business: now the two of them just had to prove they could hit it off as a top-class partnership. Once again the eyes of the footballing world were on Luis Suarez – and the big Geordie who had been brought in to ease his load up front. Their success, or failure, would go a long way towards deciding the future of the man who had paid a small fortune to bring the duo to Anfield. Suarez and Carroll owed King Kenny – he had put his reputation on the line for them.

CHAPTER SIX

THE MAGNIFICENT SEVEN

A few days after Luis's arrival at Anfield, I asked someone close to the club how he was settling in. 'Really well,' I was told. 'He is a nice guy who is working hard to integrate with the squad and is keen to get a hundred per cent fit and show what he can do. And the really great thing is that he is grateful to be here; he really loves Liverpool and knows all about the history of the club.'

'Oh yeah,' I replied, unable to conceal the scepticism in my tone. 'Next thing, he'll be kissing the badge and saying how he always wanted to play for Liverpool – that it was always his ambition from childhood!'

'Well,' the inside man said, smiling, 'he's already said that! And I believe him. He knew all about our European Cup wins and our big players through the last couple of decades and the managers too – from Shankly to Kenny. Thing is, you see, when he was ten or eleven, he used to play on his PlayStation as Liverpool, always Liverpool. We became his English club and he learned all about us on the Internet.

'He truly has the club at heart and wants to become a legend here, like Kenny and others he mentioned, including Rushy and Keegan.'

I nodded, impressed. The boy clearly meant business and wasn't just another of the badge kissers I'd come across at other big clubs; the 'talk the talk' brigade. No, according to the inside men at Anfield, it sounded as if Luis Suarez already had Liverpool in his heart and was determined to make his name in its history; to become a modern-era part of the legendary club he had learned about on his PlayStation and the Internet.

Soon enough he would get his chance to make a start on that journey. Already, of course, he had taken charge of the iconic number-seven shirt – and both fans and pundits hoped he would grace it better than some other recent incumbents. The shirt had remained unused in the dressing room since Robbie Keane's disappointing six-month spell at Liverpool in the 2008/09 season. And, as the *Liverpool Echo* pointed out, 'Suarez – the current Dutch Footballer of the Year – will be hoping to follow in the footsteps of the likes of Kevin Keegan, Peter Beardsley and current manager Kenny Dalglish, all of whom starred for the Reds wearing seven during the club's most successful era. The likes of Keane, Nigel Clough and Harry Kewell enjoyed markedly less successful spells... Reds fans will be hoping Suarez can now add his name to the list of magnificent sevens to have lit up Anfield over the years.'

Lifelong Liverpool fan Roy Stone summed up the feelings of most supporters when he said,

I hope he fills the shirt rather than just scampers about in it like some of the more recent players who took it on. If he does anywhere near as good as Kenny or Keegan, we'll all be delighted. He seems to be a goal-scorer – if his record in Holland is anything to go by – but his disciplinary record is a worry. Kenny rarely missed matches – I hope Luis can keep a lid on his temper and do his talking on the pitch. If he wants to become a Liverpool legend, he needs to sort his head out and concentrate on his work on Saturday afternoons.

It was an interesting comment. The fans were clearly looking forward to Suarez bringing them goals – and lots of them – but they were also worried about what they had heard of his bust-ups in Holland. It was true: however brilliant a player and a goal-scorer he was, he wouldn't be able to deliver the goods if he was up in the stands, serving bans every other week.

Another fan, Ben, said, 'Suarez is a young exciting talent who will frighten defenders with his pace & skills! I predict a very bright future for our new number seven.'

And, tongue-in-cheek, Liverpool fan Danny added, with the upcoming match against Chelsea and their new signing Fernando Torres in mind, 'Good luck, Luis, you are welcome to bite Torres on Sunday!'

Before that, Luis would make his debut against Stoke, on 2 February 2011. Because of his ban in Amsterdam over the biting incident, he would be ring-rusty; he hadn't played in a competitive match for over two months but he was raring to go when Dalglish told him he would make his debut at the Potteries club. Luis said, 'I am happy already here. It is important for anybody to go to such a big club. It is a great opportunity for me. It is a beautiful club. Everybody wants to play there. They always play Champions League or Europa League and belong to the top four clubs in the Premier League.'

Luis walked out proudly with the Liverpool team for the Stoke match at Anfield. He raised his right arm to salute the Kop and they immediately replied as one, applauding and singing his name, even though he would start the match on the sidelines. It wouldn't be long before they had come up with a song dedicated to him, which they would sing often and passionately. To the tune of Depeche Mode's 'Just Can't Get Enough', the Kop would acclaim their new hero with the words,

> His name is Suarez, he wears the famous Red,
> I just can't get enough, I just can't get enough.
> When he scores a volley or when he scores a head,
> I just can't get enough, I just can't get enough.
> He scores a goal and the Kop go wild,
> And I just can't seem to get enough Suarez,
> Do-do-do-do-do-do-do,
> Do-do-do-do-do-do-do,
> Do-do-do-do-do-do-do,
> Luis Suarez!

And Suarez would get off to a flier in his Liverpool career, scoring on his debut as they comfortably beat Stoke 2–0. Raul Meireles put the hosts ahead just after the interval and Luis was on hand to make it 2–0 after almost eighty minutes. He had come off the substitutes' bench seventeen minutes earlier to more applause and goodwill from all sides of the ground. 'It really helped me feel at home when the fans clapped me,' he told a friend after the match. 'I had been a bit nervous but they settled me. And after I scored, I had a good feeling that everything would be just fine – that the fans would always support me if I worked hard and kept knocking in the goals for them.'

As goals go, it was a simple one for Luis. He collected the ball, darted inside the box, rounded Stoke keeper Asmir Begovic and flashed it home, beyond the legs of the despairing last-man defender, Andy Wilkinson.

Afterwards, a beaming Dalglish said, 'Great start for Luis; he took his goal well and will get better and better as he gains full fitness. It has been a busy week and we've been in the newspapers more than we would have liked to have been. It is great credit to Luis and the other players that they have not let it get to them and they've gone out and been magnificent. The supporters realise that there is a great group here who want to compete for everything and get as much as we can from every game.'

The Liverpool manager was licking his lips at the prospect of Suarez when he eventually lined up with Andy Carroll, as well as the attacking instincts of Steven Gerrard and Meireles. Dalglish added, '[With the four of them] you are starting to frighten some of the opposition. They are four fantastic players. Andy is going to be a few weeks away from being fit but we bought him for five and a half years so a few weeks out of that won't do us any harm. Those four are really good footballers and they will complement each other very well.'

Dalglish then told Sky Sports,

[Luis] Suarez scored on his debut, which is fantastic for him and great for the supporters and everyone. He's not trained with the players yet because of the paperwork that had to be finished. He only got his work permit yesterday. He's not trained but it's something to look forward to when he starts training with the lads.

It's a clean sheet and it's the best team we had at our disposal so we had to play with what we had that best suited us and I thought that was the best way to do it. We had to compete against their strengths and try and get our own game going and we did compete against them and we did get our own game going. It's great credit to the players, I'm really pleased. It's great that Luis scored on his debut – he worked hard and I'm really pleased for him.

The fans were also excited by Suarez's performance and what he would bring to the team when he was fully fit and integrated. One said, 'Luis Suarez already looking like a great prospect. A goal on his debut and some great touches and play, he was like a skilful little firecracker out there. Then Kenny comes out and says that was the first time he'd even played with the squad!'

Even rival Stoke boss, Tony Pulis, admitted he was 'happy for Suarez'! There had been some contention that Luis's goal was actually an own goal by Wilkinson; some pundits felt he had helped the ball on its way into the net and that Suarez should not have stolen the glory. But Pulis said, 'If I was Kenny, if he [Suarez] was half a yard anywhere near the ball, I'd be saying it was his goal. We are quite happy for the lad to have it. I watched him in the World Cup and in games for Ajax and he's a wonderful player – but give him a bit of time.'

Suarez declared himself 'delighted' with his contribution and the goal that made his debut 'a dream' one. He thanked the Liverpool fans for their immediate backing and also had the good grace to send a message of thanks to the fans at Ajax who had stood by him through thick and thin during his time in Amsterdam. Writing on his official website, Luis said,

I want to thank Ajax for those wonderful 3 years and a half I spent in Amsterdam, where I've been so happy and pride [sic] to wear and defend Ajax colours. Special thanks to all my fans for supporting me and to all people who helped me during last years. I will always have you guys in my heart. I am starting a new adventure now with a very important club. I want to thank them for the strong effort they've done to count on me. I am going to work hard day by day to give them back the trust they have in me.

Three days later and Luis was on the subs' bench yet again, as Liverpool travelled to west London to take on Chelsea at

Stamford Bridge. This time he would not take a bow and would not be the star attraction. As Luis watched from the bench, Torres made a poor start to his Chelsea career as their record £50 million signing. He was, naturally enough, given a hard time of it by the Liverpool fans in the away end, who had been sickened by his demands for a move to London. They had thought he was loyal to the Scouse cause but in the end money and the prospect of easier silverware had turned the big Spaniard's head.

So it was with some glee that the Kop fans at the Bridge that day revelled in Torres's discomfort. It was the first time he would struggle in the blue shirt of Chelsea but it would be far from the last, as he continually failed to live up to his billing as one of the world's most fearsome strikers. Indeed, after he left Liverpool, Torres's form went downhill – and quickly too. He was never again the player he had been in his prime at Anfield: the hitman who had given Man United's Nemanja Vidic, one of the Premier League's toughest defenders, regular nightmares when up against him.

No, the new Torres couldn't have hit a barn door, let alone a goal from five yards. His debut for Chelsea against his old club suggested he might struggle – and so it proved. For Luis that day, there was only joy that his new club triumphed 1–0, a win that had them still just bubbling under the top four. I was told after the game that Dalglish was determined to adopt a 'softly-softly' approach with Luis. That he knew the player would need time to build up his fitness and stamina again after being out of action since the beginning of December; that he had bought him – and Andy Carroll – for the long-term, so why gamble with Luis's fitness now, when any setback could see him sidelined for weeks with Carroll?

Liverpool skipper Gerrard agreed with King Kenny's approach. He said, even after working for just a few days with Luis, he recognised that the player was naturally talented and felt, like Kenny, that he would be a force to be reckoned with once he hit peak fitness. Gerrard said,

Already we can see what a good player Luis is. He's got good pace and awareness and he's settled in very quickly. He's a fighter too and the type of character he is means he's going to work really hard for the team. We've all been delighted with his first few performances. Hopefully there is even more to come from him too. I expect him to be even better when he adjusts to the speed of football in this country. He hadn't played many games in the weeks before he moved here so he's still getting his match fitness. When he gets that, he will be very difficult to stop.

It wasn't long before Dalglish let him off the leash again and this time decided he was worth his full debut against Wigan at Anfield. Luis did not let him down; only the post denied him two goals in front of an impressed Kop. A 1–1 draw was a poor result for Liverpool. Dalglish was aiming for a top-four finish at the end of the season but knew he would have to beat the likes of Wigan at home if that were to be achieved. A goal from Meireles had put Liverpool ahead but Steve Gohouri swooped to equalise and earn Latics an unlikely point.

Afterwards Dalglish could not hide his disappointment at the draw. He said,

Obviously we are disappointed not to take the three points and with a bit of luck maybe we would have, despite the performance not being as good as it has been in the past. I think there were three or four occasions in the first half we would have been in but the sharpness was just missing a bit, which is understandable.

I think Wigan may have been a bit aggrieved if they had gone away without a point but Luis hit the post twice and their goal was offside – these things happen. We just have to brush ourselves down and get on with it. It's not been too damaging. We'll keep going.

But he had words of encouragement – and praise – for his new Uruguayan hitman. He said, 'Luis loves to score goals and was unlucky not to get on the scoresheet. In normal circumstances maybe we would have taken him off because he's not had a game for a while. It probably pushed him that bit too far. We were just hoping he might get us a goal.'

Luis also played in the next match – a 3–1 loss at West Ham – but it was the game after that he had been most looking forward to when he arrived in England: yes, Liverpool's home clash with their bitterest rivals, Manchester United. 'He knew all about Manchester United – their history and how they were one of the most famous teams in the world,' a source close to Suarez told me. 'But he also knew all about Liverpool's rivalry with United and how much it meant to the club and the fans to beat them. It had always been his aim to be picked for the United match – he saw it as a chance to make himself an almost instant hero with the Kop by scoring against them – hopefully, the winning goal.'

Well, Luis did make the starting eleven against the Red Devils but he would not make it on to the scoresheet. A Dirk Kuyt hat-trick killed off United with Javier Hernandez grabbing United's consolation. But Luis did have the first laugh: it was his brilliance that set up Dutchman Kuyt for the opener. He dribbled past Rafael, Michael Carrick and Wes Brown and then threaded a wonderful ball through the legs of United keeper Edwin van der Sar, which Kuyt prodded home.

The defeat rankled so much with United that boss Alex Ferguson refused to talk to the press after the match. But Dalglish was more than happy to chat – and to pay tribute to Luis, who had shown many glimpses of the skill that would lighten up Anfield over the coming years. Kenny said,

The players deserve fantastic credit for how they went about their jobs. The referee had an easy game to manage apart from a couple of incidents. The quality of the football was the most important thing for me and the attention should be on that. Both sets of players deserve great credit.

Dirk got three goals for us and he will get the headlines and Luis played fantastically well but the rest of them were not too far behind. The way they went about their job, their attitude, their commitment, their desire to get a result, the pride they showed in playing for the football club and the pride they showed in their own performances: that is the reason why they got the result. Without everyone giving everything they have got you don't beat Manchester United – and they did that.

Luis's next learning curve in English football came when Liverpool travelled to Sunderland on 20 March 2011. He grabbed his second goal for the club – but also picked up his first booking – at the same time helping Liverpool to a 2–0 victory. There was another first within the mix: the first time he had started for the club in tandem with £35 million buy Andy Carroll. The former Newcastle striker had come on as a 74th-minute sub in the previous match against Man United, to deafening applause from the Kop, and now he was aiming to make up for lost time by developing his partnership with Suarez.

There were encouraging signs as the duo dovetailed in attack, with Carroll's presence creating vital space for Luis and his headed knockdowns from set pieces offering opportunities for the smaller Uruguayan to feed on. It was almost two months since they had both joined Liverpool, so it was easy to understand Carroll's almost over-enthusiasm as he battered his way through the Sunderland defence. Here was a man determined to make up for lost time and to prove that he could play well enough and score enough goals to justify that mighty transfer fee.

Liverpool had gone ahead thanks to a Kuyt penalty conversion, after John Mensah brought down Jay Spearing. Suarez sealed victory with his goal fifteen minutes from time – and a beauty it was too. He ran towards the goal and dispatched the ball into the net from the tightest of angles at the byline, past the bemused keeper, Simon Mignolet.

Later boss Dalglish was still purring at Luis's divine contribution and said, 'Luis's goal was simply stunning – and, overall, it was a great effort from our players – we deserved the victory. It is great credit to the players and their determination.'

I was told that Suarez was also bubbling after his wonder goal. 'In the dressing room after the game, he couldn't stop smiling,' a source said. 'He loved being praised by the other players and you could see a bond starting to form. On the coach home, he was on the phone to his wife, excitedly telling her about his goal and the night's proceedings. It was a bit of a breakthrough, that goal – it showed just what a genius Luis was, how he could do things with the ball that others could only dream of doing. If they hadn't known it before, Liverpool's players now knew they had a footballing genius in their midst.'

The fans were delighted and full of awe too. One Liverpool supporter said, 'Suarez, what a player! That was some goal. A great buy. We're still a two-man team – only this time it's Meireles and Suarez. Andy Carroll, so far, is really only useful at set pieces, knock-ons and winning second balls. We need wingers to get anything from him. I didn't see him gel with Suarez, so far Carroll looking like an expensive purchase and I must say never been fan of these types of forwards – like Crouch, Heskey, Žigić and Dzeko.'

Another Reds fan added, 'Fernando who? Suarez has settled

faster than any striker since the great Spaniard came to Anfield at the same age. Love his tenacity, desire and overall play. The corner from which Carroll's header was cleared on the line was won by Suarez's battling from a nothing situation. His overall movement and out-sized strength will create problems for every opposition's defence.'

That latter comment would prove visionary: Suarez would be every Premier League club's nightmare in the years to come.

But one fan of football, not Liverpool, could not resist putting a cheeky boot in on the club's celebrations, saying, 'Suarez looks too good for Liverpool. Would love to see how he would do with a better team like Real. Pretty sure that he has his heart set on Spain. Once other teams begin to see how effective he's been playing for a substandard English team, he'll be gone.'

It was a cynical, mocking comment from a fan of another football team. But it held some possible truths: basically, that Suarez had the potential to be the best of the best and that the giants of Spanish football would come sniffing round if and when he hit his peak. Especially as his agent was Per Guardiola, the brother of then Barca boss, Pep.

So, even in his first couple of months at Anfield, it was obvious that Liverpool had signed a rare talent – a man who would be coveted by the world's biggest clubs and whom Liverpool would have to work hard to keep.

Suarez would need proof that the club had ambitions to match his own – basically that they could progress enough to make the Champions League every season. It was a big task for Dalglish and his backroom team but, as the manager said at the time, he wouldn't have spent close to £60 million for Suarez and Carroll if he hadn't targeted the Champions League as a viable prospect.

Of course, that first season at Anfield was less than half a season for Luis – from February to May – and so it would have been harsh to judge the potential of Dalglish's team in such a short space of time, or the potential of Luis. Having said that, Liverpool were clearly a much better team with Luis than they had been without him: his goal threat and general menace in attack marked them out as dangerous opposition. And the fact is this: when Luis joined the club, they were languishing in mid-table (twelfth) but, with him in the team, by the end of the season they had moved up to sixth. Not a bad finish considering this was a team in transition – an exciting transition given the attack-minded players Kenny was bringing into the club.

Arguably, his best performance in those first three months came in the 5–2 thrashing of Fulham at Craven Cottage in May, the third last game of the campaign. Luis scored the fifth goal for Liverpool, collecting the ball from Jonjo Shelvey and rounding keeper Mark Schwarzer before coolly slotting the ball home. He also set up the first goal for hat-trick hero Maxi Rodriguez and generally led the Fulham backline a merry dance. It was a superb, all-round showing by the man Liverpool fans had by now taken to their hearts. He ran the show for Dalglish and the manager shook his head in awe at the post-match press conference and smiled, saying, 'Luis was fantastic. He was running as hard at the end as at the beginning. Even in our wildest dreams we couldn't have thought he'd settle as well as he has done. He has graced the pitch every time he has stepped on it.

'It was a fantastic result and performance. Fulham have got a great record here and you always expect a difficult game at Craven Cottage. To score five goals is beyond our expectations. We are delighted.'

The *Guardian*'s David Hytner best summed up the influence Suarez had had at Liverpool by saying,

Were the club really languishing in 12th place in the Premier League when he [Dalglish] took over in January? There are many differences between then and now, principally in terms of confidence and a feel-good factor. But, perhaps above all, there is Luis Suarez, the £22.7 million winter window signing from Ajax. It takes something to eclipse the achievement of a hat-trick from a team-mate and nothing ought to be taken away from Maxi Rodriguez, who was in ruthless mood and reached his personal landmark with a beauty from distance. But Suarez managed it. He was irrepressible, leaving Fulham's defenders dazed and confused and proving the architect of his club's latest resounding win...

Liverpool fans were also quick to laud Suarez. One said, 'The best bit of transfer business in the Premier League this year by far is "Suarez in and Torres out". He has a load more to offer than Torres, cost half the price and – so far – is not a prima donna. He works his socks off for 90 plus minutes, sets up goals, scores them and creates plenty of space for the other attackers. Can't wait to see him and Stevie G running things up front.'

Another said, 'It's difficult to know whether it's Suarez or Dalglish who has been the catalyst for the recent revival of Liverpool, but if the club manage to bring in a couple of decent signings over the summer and they get a bit of luck next season, then it could be "squeaky bum" time once again.'

Even a fan of Liverpool's biggest rivals piped up to praise Luis Suarez. Malcolm Bowman said, 'I support United, but what a player Suarez is – just brilliant.' Quite a compliment, Luis!

There had been hopes that Liverpool might even make Europe – albeit in the Europa League – at the end of Luis's first season. His own form had been remarkable given his two-month lay-off due to the suspension for biting back in Amsterdam. He had come into the team and inspired them to some seriously good results and it was suggested they might finish fifth and claim a spot in Europe.

But it wasn't to be. Suarez's first season – half-season – on Merseyside fizzled out as Liverpool lost their final two Premier League matches. They went down 2–0 at home to Tottenham, who would now go on to clinch that Europa League place, and 1–0 away at Aston Villa. The loss to Spurs was a particular disappointment for Luis as it meant the north Londoners now leapfrogged them into fifth place and that European competition spot. Luis had made it clear in his early days at Anfield that he had joined Liverpool in the expectation that he would be playing in European matches. Ideally, the Champions League, although I was told he accepted it might 'take a season or two for that', given that Liverpool were essentially a club in transition when he arrived.

So it was a setback when they allowed Tottenham to usurp them. But progress had certainly been made from the mid-table position the club were in when he arrived: Luis could see that, he accepted that the club was moving forward and that better times lay ahead. The Spurs match was the first since Dalglish had moved from caretaker to full-time manager and it was hardly the ideal result from which to celebrate his new, three-year deal. The second coming of the King had been a story of success and raised expectations but now it was brought to an abrupt halt with the double losses in the final two games of the campaign.

It was an agonising afternoon for Liverpool and Suarez; indeed, some pundits argued he was lucky to escape with just a yellow card when he kicked out at Michael Dawson as his own frustrations grew.

The 1–0 loss in the last game of the season at Villa Park confirmed that Liverpool would not be playing European football the following year. It was the first time they had missed out in twelve years. Dalglish was in a typical fiery mood after the game, making it clear that the reason for the failure to qualify for European football could not be laid at his door – and, thus, indirectly blaming it on former boss Roy Hodgson.

Kenny said, 'We [didn't] not qualify for Europe because we lost a game today – it was because we had a bad start to the season. If you start as badly as that, you are lucky to be sixth, come the end of it. To get so close is a great compliment to the players. I'm disappointed we didn't finish on a high as the players have done fantastic to get as far as they have done.'

Luis was also disappointed but shrugged his shoulders when asked about it. It was one of those things – but he would certainly expect to make Europe the next time round. As he headed off home to Uruguay for a summer holiday, he reflected on a first season mini-campaign that had seen him make thirteen appearances for Liverpool – with one as sub – and score four goals. It would do for starters but there was more to come from him… Much more, as we would soon learn.

CHAPTER SEVEN

GETTING SHIRTY

I often hear the claim that Kenny Dalglish failed during his second coming as the Liverpool messiah; that he was old hat, past his sell-by date and had not moved with the times. But I must admit I still find it really hard to get my head around those allegations. For me, King Kenny DID succeed when he took over the reins again. After all, he won a trophy, got the team to a second Wembley final, had the vision to see that Jordan Henderson would be a good, solid buy – with the added advantage that he was English – and also brought in Andy Carroll... and the genius called Luis Suarez.

OK, you might argue that Carroll was a flop at Anfield considering he cost £35 million. But I would contend that Carroll COULD have been a success – that he CAN play it on the ground as well as in the air – and, anyway, he really cost minus £15 million if you accept he was brought in only when it was clear Fernando Torres wanted out to Chelsea.

And did Carroll really get a fair go of it under Brendan Rodgers? I think not – although I do also accept that, in Daniel Sturridge, Rodgers brought in a more fluid forward who could dovetail superbly with Suarez. Carroll and Suarez looked as though they could forge a Little & Large partnership but they weren't given time, as Rodgers decided to move Carroll to West Ham for a fee that would eventually touch £18 million.

However, during the year that Luis and Andy did play together, they certainly showed promise as a partnership.

Luis, Andy and Kenny would get one full season together – the 2011–12 campaign – and there would be highs and lows for all three men.

They would lift the League Cup, lose in the final of the FA Cup and finish strongly in the Premier League but Kenny would lose his job, Andy would be moved on and Luis would be involved in the unsavoury 'race incident' with Manchester United's Patrice Evra.

Luis was in a confident mood when the season began in August 2011. He had won the Player of the Tournament at the Copa America with Uruguay and also lifted the trophy after his country beat Paraguay 3–0 in the final. So when he arrived back in England with wife Sofia and daughter Delfina, he was refreshed and ready to show just why he had won that personal honour.

He told reporters he was happier than he had been for a long time and that the past year had been a brilliant one with the birth of Delfina and his move from Amsterdam to Liverpool:

> It was such an unforgettable year, one that was filled with many emotional moments, such as the World Cup and the birth of my daughter. Also, all the personal awards I received. It all means so much to me, especially at my age. Not even I believe everything that has happened to me. Everything has been so fast. Things that I never imagined at fifteen years old.
>
> I cannot stand to be without Sofia and Delfina for too long. Luckily, Delfina behaves really well on airplanes. Recently though, when we were in Uruguay, she started to fuss a bit – with the heat here and her teeth coming in. What I most enjoy about my daughter is watching her wake up. She's always very happy and when she sees us, her face lights up. They're moments that I very much enjoy. Moments that I never imagined.

But given his happiness and contentment at the start of the season, ultimately it would turn out to be a surprisingly difficult and trying campaign. There were moments that would live long in Luis's memory – the League Cup win and some superb goals. But there would also be that run-in with Evra.

His most memorable goals would come in the second half of the season. Luis would score eleven in total and grabbed his first hat-trick for the club against Norwich in April 2012. Liverpool won 3–0 in the Premier League fixture and his third goal was a classic strike from almost the halfway line as he lobbed the ball cheekily over despairing keeper John Ruddy. It was the perfect way for Luis to warm up for the imminent FA Cup final against Chelsea at Wembley.

Kop boss Dalglish was full of praise for his star man, saying, 'He's a special player. It was a fantastic performance. Everybody knows what's coming ahead on Saturday but the team did their jobs professionally and efficiently. Luis has been like that many times this year and has not been rewarded – and it's the same with the team. That third goal is not difficult to score if you've got Luis Suarez's ability – it's more difficult if you are a mere mortal. The clean sheet was also important for us. It gives the defenders and Pepe Reina a bit of a boost.'

Liverpool skipper Steven Gerrard was also eager to praise Suarez, although he did admit he was initially peeved that the Uruguayan had opted to shoot from the halfway line for that wonder goal: 'I was just about to give him a rollicking but I ended up clapping him. It was a fantastic individual performance by Luis. It was world class, so clinical. We are lucky to have him. Only certain players in the world can score goals like that third one – and he is one of them. It was about vision more than technique.'

Liverpool fans were also purring with delight at Suarez's brilliance and in bullish mood for the FA Cup final, given the Uruguayan's current form. Hassan, from London, commented, 'Just wonderful from King Kenny's boys! And sheer brilliance from Senor Suarez! On form like this you'd have to fancy them to challenge for the title next season. Looking forward to adding yet another piece of silverware to the trophy cabinet next Saturday.'

While Nieve, from Dublin, added, 'Luis is an amazing, talented player and yesterday against Norwich he was on fire. Let's hope he doubles that performance next week against Chelsea in the FA Cup final.'

Luis also excelled – and it was in tandem with Andy Carroll – as Liverpool progressed to the final. In the fifth round they hammered Brighton 6–1 to set up a quarter-final clash with Stoke City. Both Andy and Luis were on the scoresheet as Albion crumbled at Anfield, also conceding three own goals as the Suarez/Carroll partnership left them in a blind panic. Luis even missed from the penalty spot after Brighton substitute Craig Noone had fouled Dirk Kuyt. But he headed home Liverpool's sixth goal after Carroll set him up for it.

It was the first time that Luis, Andy and Steven Gerrard had started a match together and the combination of the three proved lethal as they swamped their desperate visitors. The trio had played just sixty-nine minutes on the same field and Dalglish now said he was 'very keen' for them to do more damage:

Someone said they'd played sixty-nine minutes before so I assumed they must have started somewhere – but they hadn't. The more anybody or any team gets the players that are iconic like they are on the pitch, the better chance they've got of being successful. But we've got more than three players and the fact that we've done as well as we have and that's the first time they've all started a match tells you how well the rest of the boys have done as well.

We'll stand and be counted as a squad and I don't think we've done too badly this year.

Carroll's goal against Brighton was only his eighth since his £35 million move to Anfield thirteen months previously. But Dalglish made it clear he was happy with the big striker and how he was starting to develop a partnership with Luis. The manager added, 'We've always been positive and we always will be and we'll always be supportive of any player that comes to this football club. It doesn't matter what his name is, we'll judge him and we'll judge whether we're happy or unhappy.'

Another high point for Luis that season came at Wembley at the end of February when he lifted his first trophy with Liverpool – the League Cup, also known as the Carling Cup. Liverpool were up against Championship outfit Cardiff. The Reds started as clear favourites, given they were a division above the Welsh side, but they needed a penalty shootout to win the trophy after a gallant display by the underdogs.

Liverpool won 3–2 on penalties to lift their first trophy since their FA Cup triumph in 2006. Luis had played well and almost scored Liverpool's first goal, only to be denied by a post, with Martin Skrtel then forcing the ball home. Afterwards Dalglish was also jubilant and said he believed this was the start of something big for the club: 'Although we have won something today, that is not us finished. We don't want to stop here. We want to keep going. We've won it and we are going to really enjoy it. I know how much the players have enjoyed it and it gives you a wee flavour to come back and do it again.'

Liverpool sub Kuyt admitted that he and the likes of Suarez had been determined to win their first medals at the club: 'We wanted this so desperately. This is why we came to Anfield. To get a first medal is great.'

Luis celebrated with the team at their victory party after the win and then it was back down to business. A couple of months later he would be back at Wembley as Liverpool took on Chelsea in the FA Cup final. But this time there would be no happy ending, as the Blues won 2–1 with goals from Ramires and Didier Drogba. The only slight consolation for Luis was that his strike partner Carroll scored Liverpool's goal just after the hour mark.

Suarez was 'gutted' by the defeat – especially as he believed he had set up Carroll for an equaliser as Liverpool bombarded the Chelsea goal late on. Luis crossed and Carroll headed home what looked to be a certain goal but Chelsea keeper Petr Cech was alert enough to push the ball on to the bar.

Dalglish praised his players, saying, 'They've been in two cup finals in this season – they'll have enjoyed the first one more than the second. The lads will benefit from the experience. You can't give a team like Chelsea a two-goal head start. They were the best team for the first hour but we finished strongly and maybe if we'd started that way, we'd be happier than we are now.'

Speaking about the late Cech save, Carroll paid tribute to Suarez for setting him up and added, 'I thought it was over the line and you know better than me but I thought it was. I thought it hit the other side of the bar but I haven't seen it back. I had a few chances and could have put them away but it wasn't to be. We came here to win, it's been disappointing in the league, we got here and it was unlucky because it would have taken us into extra time. I did the best I could when I came on and we were unlucky.'

Dalglish had spoken as if he expected to have the chance to further develop the players he had bought into a more efficient unit. But the club's American owners wanted league success – they wanted Liverpool back in the Champions League. That was more important than winning the Carling Cup or playing in the final of the FA Cup.

Liverpool finished the season in eighth place in the Premier League, thirty-four points behind Manchester United and Manchester City and eighteen behind Arsenal. That would be the ultimate yardstick by which the legendary Dalglish would now be judged: the owners decided he had failed and, shortly after the FA Cup final, sacked the Liverpool legend.

It left Luis sickened and upset: he had grown to admire Kenny and had a close relationship with him, as shown when Dalglish had backed him in his race row with Evra. However, that controversy hadn't helped the manager in persuading the owners to keep him on: indeed, in the minds of many pundits it had contributed to his downfall.

The incident had certainly ruined Luis's season and, many would argue, his reputation in England. It would end with the FA declaring Suarez guilty of racially abusing Evra and being handed an eight-game suspension and a £40,000 fine.

It all blew up when Liverpool played host to Manchester United in a Premier League match on 15 October 2011. Liverpool had taken the lead through a Steven Gerrard free kick, only for Javier Hernandez to equalise for United. After the game – which ended in a 1–1 draw – Liverpool boss Dalglish spoke of his delight at his team's performance and, in particular, praised the impact of Suarez and Gerrard. He said,

It's a real indication of how far these players have come that they are sitting in the dressing room disappointed they have drawn with Manchester United. Their attitude, even when United equalised, was admirable as they came back and went for the three points. The only thing missing from the performance was that we are not walking away with three points. We are running out of vocabulary to describe Luis Suarez. He is a fantastic footballer and has been so since he has come here. I'm sure he will continue to be that.

The fact we have got Steven Gerrard playing is a real boost for us and it is fantastic he crowned his first start for a while by scoring. He has made a fantastic contribution to this club and will continue to do so. To see him back is brilliant for us but, even more importantly, brilliant for him.

Dalglish's comments showed he was unaware of the claims that were to follow: at the time, he had no idea that his star player and Liverpool FC were about to become embroiled in a damaging race row. Suarez would soon face accusations of racially abusing United's French fullback Patrice Evra. It started to make headlines a day later, after Evra reported the incident and the FA confirmed they would be looking into his allegations. The two players had been seen bickering throughout the match but there had been nothing to suggest that any racial abuse had taken place.

But at the end of the ninety minutes Evra told the match referee, Andre Marriner, that he had been the victim of racial abuse. He was then quoted as telling French TV station Canal Plus, 'There are cameras, you can see him [Suarez] say a certain word to me at least ten times.'

An FA statement read, 'Referee Andre Marriner was made aware of an allegation at the end of the fixture and has reported this to the FA.' It added, 'The FA will now begin making enquiries into the matter.'

But a Liverpool spokesman said Suarez 'categorically denied' the allegation.

Luis also wrote on his Twitter and Facebook pages that he was upset by the accusation and denied the claims. Suarez tweeted, 'I can only say that I have always respected and respect everybody. We are all the same. I go to the field with the maximum illusion of a little child who enjoys what he does, not to create conflicts.'

As the FA conducted their investigation, Liverpool and United said they would stay silent but that was easier said than done. United boss Alex Ferguson, Dalglish and Suarez all made comments in the month it took the FA to come to a decision on the case.

On 17 October Ferguson said, 'We spoke to Patrice today and he's adamant that he wants to follow it on. It's not an easy one because everyone knows that United and Liverpool have great responsibilities in terms of what happens on the field.

Obviously, Patrice feels very aggrieved at what was said to him and it rests with the FA now.'

On 28 October Dalglish said, 'We would rather have it done and dusted, out in the open. Whoever is the guilty party – the person who said it or the accuser – should get their due punishment.'

And on 8 November Luis also spoke out, saying, 'The FA will have to clarify things. There is no evidence I said anything racist to him. I said nothing of the sort. There were two parts of the discussion, one in Spanish, one in English. I did not insult him. It was just a way of expressing myself. I called him something his team-mates at Manchester call him and even they were surprised by his reaction.'

Boss Dalglish also took to Twitter to say he was 'very disappointed' and that 'this is the time when Luis Suarez needs our full support. Let's not let him walk alone.'

Almost a month after the incident, the FA finally announced they would be charging Luis with 'abusive and/or insulting words and/or behaviour contrary to FA rules', including 'a reference to the ethnic origin and/or colour and/or race of Patrice Evra'.

Liverpool swiftly released their own statement, making it clear they believed Luis to be innocent and saying they would stand by him. The statement read, 'The club this afternoon received notification from the Football Association of their decision to charge Luis Suarez and will take time to review properly the documentation which has been sent to us. We will discuss the matter fully with him when he returns from international duty, but he will plead not guilty to the charge and we expect him to request a personal hearing.

'Luis remains determined to clear his name of the allegation made against him by Patrice Evra. The club remain fully supportive of Luis in this matter.'

Two months after the incident – on 20 December 2011 – the FA concluded a seven-day hearing and finally came to their conclusion with that eight-match ban and £40,000 fine. Luis was told he had fourteen days to appeal against the decision. He said on Twitter, 'Today is a very difficult and painful day for me and my family. Thanks for all the support.'

Liverpool FC issued a full statement expressing their disappointment at the decision. It read,

We find it extraordinary that Luis can be found guilty on the word of Patrice Evra alone. No one else on the field of play – including Evra's own Manchester United team-mates and all the match officials – heard the alleged conversation between the two players in a crowded Kop goalmouth. It appears to us that the FA were determined to bring charges against Luis Suarez, even before interviewing him at the beginning of November.

Nothing we have heard in the course of the hearing has changed our view that Luis Suarez is innocent of the charges brought against him and we will provide Luis with whatever support he now needs to clear his name.

It was a strong response from the club but they then went even further by suggesting the FA should also charge Evra for making abusive remarks to an opponent. The statement added, 'Evra admitted himself in his evidence to insulting Luis

Suarez in Spanish in the most objectionable of terms. Luis, to his credit, actually told the FA he had not heard the insult.'

Just before Christmas 2011, Ferguson again spoke out about the incident, making it clear he felt Luis had got the punishment he deserved – and mentioning how Evra himself was banned after a run-in with a groundsman at Chelsea. Ferguson said,

> We're satisfied they made the right decision. Our support of Patrice was obvious right from the word go and that's still the same. This wasn't about Manchester United and Liverpool. It was nothing to do with that. This was an individual situation where one person was racially abused.
>
> Patrice got that suspension for the incident down at Chelsea when no one was there, just a groundsman and our fitness coach. He got a four-match ban and we had to wait two weeks for the evidence to come through. We were quite astounded at that. A four-match ban? We thought it was well over the top for a trivial incident. But it happened and there's nothing you can do about it.

That appeared to be the end of the matter. Luis and Liverpool decided not to appeal and peace broke out... for a while. Then, in February 2012, the matter flared up again when Luis avoided shaking Evra's hand before the Premier League match against United at Old Trafford. Dalglish was initially angered by questioning after the match over the lack of the handshake. But the following day both he and Suarez issued apologies, which, it was claimed, had been forced upon them by the club's owners.

'I have spoken with the manager since the game at Old Trafford and I realise I got things wrong,' Suarez said. 'I have not only let the manager down but also the club and what it stands for and I'm sorry. I made a mistake and I regret what happened. I should have shaken Patrice Evra's hand before the game and I want to apologise for my actions. I would like to put this whole issue behind me and concentrate on playing football.'

And Dalglish said, 'All of us have a responsibility to represent this club in a fit and proper manner. That applies equally to me as Liverpool manager. When I went on TV after yesterday's game I hadn't seen what had happened, but I did not conduct myself in a way befitting of a Liverpool manager during that interview and I'd like to apologise for that.'

Liverpool managing director Ian Ayre also released a statement, which read,

We are extremely disappointed Luis Suarez did not shake hands with Patrice Evra before yesterday's game. The player had told us beforehand that he would, but then chose not to do so. He was wrong to mislead us and wrong not to offer his hand to Patrice Evra. He has not only let himself down but also Kenny Dalglish, his team-mates and the club.

It has been made absolutely clear to Luis Suarez that his behaviour was not acceptable. Luis Suarez has now apologised for his actions, which was the right thing to do. However, all of us have a duty to behave in a responsible manner and we hope he now understands what is expected of anyone representing Liverpool Football Club.

To which Dalglish added, 'Ian Ayre has made the club's position absolutely clear and it is right that Luis Suarez has now apologised for what happened at Old Trafford. To be honest, I was shocked to hear that the player had not shaken hands having been told earlier in the week that he would do.'

My take on the incident was that Luis had NOT set out to racially abuse Evra and that it was a confusion of a term that was acceptable in Uruguay but not in England. Of course, I am in no way defending what Luis did but I do believe he is no racist – and the players I have spoken to in the game back that up.

The issue was to rear its ugly head once more, though. In February 2014, in an interview with radio station Sport 890AM, Luis said,

Let me tell you, I've made only two mistakes in my career. My first was when I was playing for Ajax and I bit an opponent. My second was when I bit [Branislav] Ivanovic [against Chelsea]. The case with Evra was all false. I was accused without proof. But that's in the past. I was sad at that moment but I'm happy today. I have grown up. I have thought more about things before doing them.

Now people in England can't talk about me because

I'm not doing anything wrong. They have to talk about me only as a footballer. I said I'm sorry [after the Ivanovic bite] and that was all, end of story. I've nothing else to regret. All the other things were like a movie that people in England believed in.

Luis made it clear that he considered both incidents (the Ivanovic and Evra) were in the past and that he had moved on from them. Indeed, he admitted his biggest worry in February 2014 was whether he would stay free from injury so that he could compete in the World Cup, using the examples of Radamel Falcao and Theo Walcott to express his fears, as both looked to have their World Cup hopes ended by knee injuries. Luis said, 'The truth is that I am scared of what happened to Falcao and Walcott. But you live in the present and you always give your best for your club – you can't be thinking about that all the time. It is a unique opportunity and we all want to be there but I prefer to focus my mind on the English league. The moment to think about the national team will arrive later.'

Inevitably, some media outlets claimed that Suarez should be investigated by the FA over his claims about the Evra ban. But, fortunately, common sense prevailed on this occasion and the matter was forgotten. Clearly, though, it would be best for Suarez if he avoided the temptation to tread back on controversies from the past if he doesn't want the muck raking to begin again – and I was informed that his agent, Per Guardiola, had a quiet word to stress to him that silence was the best option.

However, what had started out as a potential season of

achievement but had rapidly spiralled into one of aggravation and stagnation continued on its downward trend when Luis was banned for one match for making an obscene gesture towards Fulham fans. He admitted a charge of improper conduct after he was photographed making the gesture to the home supporters after the 1–0 defeat at Craven Cottage on 5 December.

The FA issued a statement on the latest ban that said, 'Luis Suarez will begin a one-match suspension with immediate effect after he admitted an FA charge of improper conduct in relation to the same game. Suarez was also fined £20,000 and warned as to his future conduct following a gesture he made towards the Fulham fans at the end of the fixture.'

By now Luis, the fans and Liverpool FC believed the striker was the victim of a witch-hunt but they sensibly stayed silent over the latest punishment – although it meant that Luis would now miss almost half of the club's remaining fixtures that season.

There were now continued rumours that Suarez would leave Liverpool in the summer of 2012; that he was worn down and depressed by the constant spotlight on his every move and that he would prefer to make a new start and play in Spain. In the 2011–12 season he had played in 39 matches for Liverpool and scored 17 goals.

But there were signs that he did not actually want to leave England; that he felt he had unfinished business to prove to his critics that he was a great player and to show loyalty back to Liverpool and the fans who had stood by him through his several run-ins with authority. In March 2012, for example, he spoke of his desire to see out his contract at Anfield. He told the club's website, 'There are a good few years left on my contract. I want to carry on enjoying myself because both my family and I feel really happy here. I have spoken with people at the club and they know that I want to stay and that I am enjoying myself and am very happy here.'

And as the season ended for Liverpool after that FA Cup final loss to Chelsea, it would not be Suarez who would exit – instead his manager Dalglish would be the fall guy and his co-striker Andy Carroll would not be far behind him out of the door. The King's second coming came to an end on 16 May – two days after Liverpool's American owners met with him to analyse the season's successes and failures. Under Dalglish, Liverpool had won the Carling Cup, got to the final of the FA Cup and finished eighth in the Premier League. It was the Premier League 'failure' that cost Kenny his job, alongside the fallout from the Suarez/Evra bust-up. Many pundits felt Kenny had not acted correctly in continuing to defend Luis as the FA contemplated what action to take. He was especially criticised for defending his players when they warmed up for a Premier League game at Wigan wearing T-shirts featuring a picture of the Uruguayan on the front and his name and number seven on the back.

The Liverpool players had put out a statement, saying, 'We totally support Luis and we want the world to know that. We know he is not racist. We have lived, trained and played with Luis for almost 12 months and we don't recognise the way he has been portrayed. We will continue to support Luis through this difficult period, and, as a popular and respected friend of all his team-mates, he will not walk alone.'

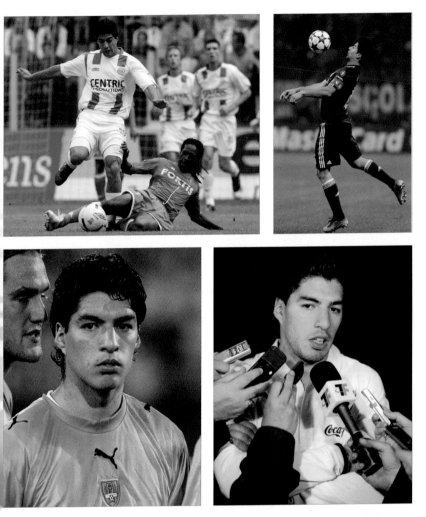

Above left: Suarez began his European football career with Groningen in 2006 when, still a teenager, he was spotted by some travelling scouts while playing in his native Uruguay.

©Getty Images

Above right: At Ajax, Suarez proved that he wouldn't be out of place on the pitch with the best in Europe, helping Ajax to domestic honours and, here, to a 2–0 away win over AC Milan in the Champions League.

©OLIVER MORIN/AFP/Getty Images

Below left: A very youthful Suarez made his debut for Uruguay in a 3–1 victory over Colombia. His night was soured though by a late red card for dissent.

© GERARDO GOMEZ/AFP/Getty Images

Below right: 'I made the save of the tournament' was the unapologetic statement Suarez made about his controversial handball against Ghana in the 2010 World Cup Finals. This wouldn't be the last time he would have to face the cameras to explain himself.

©ROBERTO SCHMIDT/AFP/Getty Images

A committed family man, Suarez's move to Europe was in part driven by his desire to be with his then-girlfriend, now wife, Sofia Balbi, with whom he now has two children.

Top: Since first putting on the Liverpool jersey, Suarez's goal celebrations have been a regular sight at Anfield.

© *Getty Images*

Middle left: In training for his first FA Cup final, which resulted in a 2–1 defeat by Chelsea at Wembley. ©*Getty Images*

Right: After a remarkable 2013-14 season, in which he bagged thirty-one goals in thirty-three games in the Premier League, Luis took home numerous awards, including the PFA Player of the Year. ©*Getty Images*

Above: Sharing a joke with his Uruguayan teammates prior to the 2014 World Cup Finals in Brazil, which he was to have quite an effect on.

© *DANIEL GARCIA/AFP/Getty Image*

Below: After a stunning brace sank England, Suarez sank his teeth into Chiellini, which resulted in an unexpected tourist attraction on Rio de Janeiro's beaches.

© *AFP/Getty Image*

The match against Wigan finished 0–0 and Dalglish reiterated his support for Luis, saying, 'We have said we will always support him – and we will. That is not just the people at the football club, it's the people who the football club means something to. They know that Luis Suarez means a great deal to them and he has got mutual respect for the fans. There is a fantastic relationship there and nothing will break it.' That did not sit well with many pundits, who questioned whether Kenny had made a mistake and misjudged the issue. Some sections of the media also claimed that Liverpool's American owners had not been impressed by Dalglish's stance either.

After his dismissal, Kenny showed his continual loyalty to the club that was closest to his heart by saying in a statement,

It has been an honour and a privilege to have had the chance to come back to Liverpool Football Club as manager. I greatly appreciate the work that the players and all of the staff put in during my time and feel proud that we delivered the club's first trophy in six years winning the Carling Cup and came close to a second trophy in the FA Cup final.

Of course I am disappointed with results in the league, but I would not have swapped the Carling Cup win for anything as I know how much it meant to our fans and the club to be back winning trophies. Whilst I am obviously disappointed to be leaving the football club, I can say that the matter has been handled by the owners and all concerned in an honourable, respectful and dignified way and reflects on the quality of the people involved and their continued desire to move the football club forward in the same way as when they arrived here. I would like to thank all of the staff at the club for their effort and loyalty. I said when first approached about coming back as manager that I would always be of help if I can at any time and that offer remains the same. Finally, I want to put on record my heartfelt gratitude to Liverpool's fans, who have always given me and the club their unwavering support. Without them neither the club nor I would have achieved anything.

It was a dignified departure for a man who had given his all to Liverpool FC and who had, in my opinion, hardly failed. I would argue that Dalglish succeeded because he won a trophy and I believe improved league results would have happened had he been given another season. But the board had made their decision and would now begin the hunt for a younger man to take Kenny's place.

Luis was sad that the man who had steadfastly stood by him and backed him was gone. He would always say how grateful he was to Dalglish and that the manager had played a huge part in both his move to England and his staying put during the dark days. But now Kenny was gone and Luis travelled home to Montevideo for his summer holidays unsure of how the new manager might view him and whether he fitted into his plans. He needn't have worried: Brendan Rodgers not only wanted him to stay at Anfield, he planned on building his team around the boy from El Salto. But before we move on to the advent of the Rogers era at Anfield, let's slow the pace and take a look at Luis's international career – starting with his efforts and, inevitably, the controversy he stirred up at the tournament that brought him to planet football's attention: the 2010 World Cup finals in South Africa.

CHAPTER EIGHT

THE WHOLE WORLD
IN HIS HAND

There was never any doubt that Luis would be in the Uruguay squad for the 2010 World Cup. He had played an important part in his country's qualification, playing in nineteen of their twenty matches en route to the tournament, although the Uruguayan press had given him a hard time after many of the games, claiming he was not committed enough to the cause. They often compared him with fellow striker Diego Forlan, unfairly and negatively saying he did not pull his weight, unlike his compatriot.

Luis was unhappy with the criticisms but never allowed it to deter him; he knew he was giving his best and trying his damndest to get his nation to the finals. No, the only real fear he had during qualification was that the team might not actually make it to South Africa. If it was an exciting if sometimes tempestuous journey for Luis, it was also torturous

131

and demanding for the Uruguayan nation as a whole, as the team claimed an unwanted niche in the history books as the last to qualify.

Luis had often said that nothing was easy and straightforward when it came to the national team – and how right he was proved as they made a meal of qualification. After finishing fifth in the South American group table, they had headed for a play-off against Costa Rica but what should have been a fairly comfortable passage through to the finals proved anything but that.

Eventually, a 1–1 home draw with the Costa Ricans booked Luis's ticket to South Africa with a 2–1 aggregate win. 'It was very tough,' the head coach, Oscar Tabarez, admitted. 'This match mirrored the tie as a whole. I'm very happy. Fortunately, we made it, in spite of the way we did it. There is a lot to improve on. We'll do so and we'll have the World Cup to prove it. I'm very happy, mostly for the kids. The ones who are younger than eight years old have never seen this and now they can live it.'

Skipper Diego Lugano was also tired and emotional at the manner in which the team had made it through the play-offs. 'I am happy to qualify but not for the way we've clinched it. It is unbelievable that we have to suffer this way.'

And Luis told friends he was 'just relieved' to have made it to the finals, although he had 'never doubted' he and the team were good enough to make it through. Together they celebrated into the night after their win over Costa Rica and the Uruguayan nation joined them, delighted that they had finally made it to the World Cup.

There were few celebrations, however, when the draw was made. Suarez and Co. were pitched against the 1998 winners France, Mexico and the hosts, the South Africans. But the players themselves remained confident that they would do their nation proud – a belief based on the attacking trio who would lead them into the finals. Up front with Luis would be former Manchester United starlet Diego Forlan – who was now carving out a name for himself as a prolific goal-scorer with Atletico Madrid in Spain – and the brilliant centre-forward Edinson Cavani, who played his club football in Italy with Napoli.

The three men's aim was a lofty one – to bring the trophy home to Montevideo for the third time. That would take some doing – Uruguay had only featured in one final in the previous twenty years, let alone not having won the tournament since 1950. Luis knew all about the glorious history of those two triumphs – he had always taken an interest in the history of both his country's international record and the fortunes of whichever club he played for. That inquisitiveness explained his knowledge of Kenny Dalglish and the likes of Ian Rush and Bob Paisley in the annals of the record books at Anfield as he put pen to paper on his own arrival at Liverpool.

He was well aware too that Uruguay had won the first ever World Cup in 1930, held on their own soil. On a proud, hot summer's day in Montevideo they beat South American rivals Argentina 4–2 in the final. Twenty years later, they won it for the second time by overpowering hosts, Brazil, 2–1 in the final match of the tournament in front of a massive crowd of close to 174,000 at the legendary Maracana Stadium in Rio.

To emulate the achievements of such eminent forefathers would take some doing and, as the ever realistic Tabarez pointed out, the first target was to get out of a tough group. Up first for Luis and the boys was what, on paper at least, looked like the crunch match of the three: France in Cape Town. With the benefit of hindsight, head coach Tabarez would admit he overestimated the threat of the French. He set up his team to stifle the likes of Franck Ribery and Thierry Henry, leaving Cavani on the bench. But Henry also started on the bench and the French never threatened to overrun the Uruguayans: indeed, they looked a team at odds with themselves, which they were. In-fighting and internal rifts before the match had killed the confidence and unity of the team, after boss Raymond Domenech had axed Florent Malouda and Henry. Plus William Gallas was unhappy that Patrice Evra had been picked as captain ahead of him.

It meant the French – who were ranked as the second best team in the world – struggled as a side and Uruguay looked back on the match as a lost opportunity: they ended up with a point after a goalless draw but, given the rock-bottom morale of their rivals, they could have won the match had they been more positive from the off. Afterwards Tabarez admitted, 'It was a hard match and we expected that. We're more or less content with the result but not with our play. We didn't have enough of the ball. Ribery played very well and Abou Diaby brought lots of balance. He was very effective in the centre of the park and changed the midfield in a way. I don't want to say that France deserved to win though, as we kept them quiet in front of our goal.'

And Forlan, who was named Man of the Match, said, 'We

never understood how to approach this match. We had a few good chances but we were often guilty of wasting our final ball. It's a shame. I thought the match was quite even.'

The press bemoaned the fact the game had been a dull-bore draw and that Suarez had never really looked like scoring, with the BBC saying, 'Striker Suarez, with forty-nine goals in forty-eight games for Ajax last season, was all too frequently caught offside, while playmaker Ignacio Gonzalez was a peripheral figure.'

The press back in Uruguay were even more critical, with some pundits questioning whether Luis even deserved his place in the team and comparing him unfavourably to his fellow striker, Forlan. But Suarez remained his usual stoical, tough self: he had battled through many lows in his footballing career over the years, so now he just kept his head down and worked hard in training. He knew he had no divine right to start the next match but also believed that, if given the nod, he was good enough to make the difference against the South Africans in Pretoria.

Tabarez clearly felt he could be just that; the head coach ignored calls for Suarez to be dropped and started him again up front with Forlan. But this time the coach decided to be more daring – he also threw Cavani into the mix, much to Luis's delight. 'Luis had always believed that a three-man attack of himself, Diego and Edinson would cause havoc among any defence,' one commentator said. 'And so it proved against the South Africans. They simply could not cope with Luis's pace, Cavani's strength and Diego's ability to sniff out goals from the slightest opportunity.'

Forlan made the headlines with two of the goals as the hosts crashed 3–0. One was a fine solo effort, the other from the penalty spot after Suarez was brought down in the box. Luis also contributed to the third goal, setting up Alvaro Pereira for an easy tap-in. The win silenced the usually boisterous South African fans, who were now facing up to the harsh reality that their team was heading out of the competition at the first hurdle.

But for Luis, victory was sweet. He had justified the faith shown by the coach in sticking by him, despite the sniping from the pundits back home in Montevideo. He had made two goals and generally proved to be a real handful for the struggling Boks' defence. The three-man attack had done all it had been asked to do and was also doing a fine job in dismantling the traditional perception of the Uruguayans as being a dire, defensive outfit.

After the win Luis was bubbling and laughing with his team-mates as they headed back to their base, the Protea Hotel in Kimberley. But, like his colleagues, he was not counting his chickens yet: he knew there was work still to be done if they were to progress. In the last group match they would face the potentially much tougher task of beating Mexico.

Luis said, 'We are confident we can go forward but we also know the threat that Mexico will pose. We know we will have to be at our best to get a result against them.'

And skipper Lugano added, 'The game against Mexico will be totally different. They are an extremely strong side and to go through they'll need to come out and attack. It would be a mistake if we get too confident. We'll be looking for the win but we also know a draw will do. We are under pressure – but we are a lot better under pressure. It's in our blood and Uruguayan players always react best in the toughest of situations.'

Fellow defender Jorge Fucile added, 'We can't get too carried away. We scored three goals this time but that doesn't mean to say we'll always do that. We should celebrate this victory and then move on. The aim is to get through and, until we do that, there's no question of us relaxing.'

Goal hero Forlan also wanted to cool pre-emptive talk of progressing to the next round: 'We knew we could win this match, we made the most of our chances, defended very well, but it was a pretty even game. The people in Uruguay and the journalists can think what they want but we're not thinking about the title. We have to keep our feet on the ground, be realistic and continue to work hard.'

Meanwhile, one of Suarez's partners in crime up front, Cavani, admitted that La Celeste – the Sky Blues – were, indeed, changing perceptions with their more attacking approach. He told FIFA.com, 'We've spoken about it a lot. We want to play a more attacking, more intelligent and faster game. This is a team that likes to go on the offensive.'

After the 3–0 win, the Uruguayan press were, indeed, starting to talk about lifting the trophy. And from knocking Suarez, they were now praising him! It is amazing what one match can do for a reputation in football but Luis himself would not get carried away now that his countrymen were lauding him and his fellow strikers, Cavani and Forlan. He knew the press blew hot and cold and so continued to work hard on the training ground and to believe that the goals would soon follow for him, as well as Forlan.

It was inevitable then that he would now score the decisive goal against Mexico that would take his country into the next round, as group winners. Luis may have still had the number-nine on his back but he was all over the forward line as he searched for his first goal of the tournament. On the left, on the right and, finally, in the centre to head home in the first half from a fine cross by Cavani. It was 1–0 and Suarez and Uruguay were on their way into the last sixteen of the World Cup. The scoreline would stay the same for the remainder of the match and Luis and Co. would be joined by the Mexicans in the next round. South Africa had beaten France 2–1 in the other concluding game of the group but the victory hadn't been enough for the plucky hosts to progress. Agonisingly for the host nation, they would exit on goal difference to Mexico.

Uruguay had topped the group on seven points, with Mexico on four, South Africa on two and the under-performing French notching up just a single point. Afterwards, Luis admitted his relief that the team were not on an early plane back to Montevideo and that he had finally opened his account in the tournament. He said, 'I'm really happy, especially because I scored my first World Cup goal. It's an incredible feeling! As far as the result goes, we achieved what we set out to do, which was to qualify. It doesn't matter now who our next opponents are: we've got what it takes to keep progressing in the competition.' After a tough opening couple of games, Suarez was now on a high. He had found the form his coach had known he had all along and had won the Man of the Match award for his efforts. He was now confident and determined that the team could go further; that the last eight would not be the end of their participation.

As he said, he was also not worried about who they might now face. Coach Tabararez was equally delighted but a little more anxious about their next opponents. He said, 'If we look at what Uruguayan national teams have done at recent World Cups, we can't be anything but totally satisfied. It was clear over the course of the first phase that we're tough opponents for anybody. Our next opponents? It seems quite unlikely that it'll be Argentina but we'll have to wait and see. The most important thing is that we did our best.'

But fortune seemed to be smiling on Luis and his team-mates, as they ended up not facing Lionel Messi, Carlos Tevez and Co. but the palpably less daunting prospect of South Korea. Of course, the Koreans were no mugs – with the likes of Man United's Ji-Sung Park among their ranks – but they were hardly the nightmare scenario that the Argentines would have presented. The match would take place in Port Elizabeth and, for Luis Suarez, it was a chance to show that, yes, he had now put the early indifferent form behind him, that he had stepped up a gear and that he was one of the best footballers on the planet.

True to form, he did just that, just as he had done against the Mexicans. No one would be questioning him after this round-of-sixteen match: indeed, all the talk would be about how he had morphed into one of the tournament's stars and how the world was now at his feet; how he could now realistically expect a rush of offers for his services at club level and how Ajax would do well to hold on to him.

Luis scored both his country's goals in the 2–1 win over South Korea. His second goal came when it looked as though the initiative was slipping away from the Uruguayans and towards the Koreans. It had a calming effect on his team-mates, who had seemed to freeze when their rivals had equalised and who appeared to be bearing the full weight of previous failings by their country's footballers in World Cups.

Luis Suarez dragged his tired team-mates across the line and into the quarter-finals. Lee Chung-Yong's headed goal had cancelled out Luis's first-half strike. But with ten minutes remaining, Luis sent his country's fans crazy as he ran with the ball into the penalty area and curled it home from a ridiculously acute angle. It was a goal worthy of winning the cup itself but, for now, it would do as the goal that earned him a last-eight place in the greatest footballing event on earth.

It was a performance that earned the Ajax player his second consecutive Man of the Match award. From a quiet start in South Africa, Luis Suarez was now hitting peak form, much to the delight of all Uruguayans. His goals had taken the country to their first World Cup quarter-final appearance in forty years and he was the hero of the hour back home in Montevideo and among his native fans in South Africa.

Afterwards, at the post-match press conference, he was inevitably overjoyed and full of optimism about his country's hopes:

As a striker, you're always looking to find the net. On this occasion, the goals allowed me to help the team through – that's the most important thing. Here what mattered was reaching the quarter-finals of the World Cup. We knew it wasn't going to be easy. The early strike helped calm us down but we sat back in the second half and tried to protect the lead. That allowed Korea Republic to get on top and we were suffering for a while.

But after their equaliser we knew we had to start playing again and, luckily for us, we managed to win it.

And he couldn't help but rhapsodise about his second goal, which was arguably the pick of the World Cup so far. 'It was a good one, wasn't it?' he said. 'When I got on the ball, the only option I had was to go for goal. I wasn't trying to put it there but the funny thing is, I scored a similar goal for Ajax last year. I'm just telling you that so they don't say it was a coincidence!'

And what were his hopes now? 'We've achieved the first two of them but we need to take things game by game. The thirty-two teams that started the World Cup came to South Africa with the aim of making the final but then that number came down to sixteen and now we're in the last eight. So our objective has to be to go on and become world champions.'

As ambitions go, Luis couldn't be faulted. He wanted to be a world champion – and he seriously believed he could be. But were his team as good as Spain, or Brazil, or Argentina, or Germany?

Coach Tabarez was keen to pay tribute to his star man before they returned to their base and planned for the quarter-final clash. He said, 'That was a demonstration of temperament, maturity and class. We played better towards the end and, fortunately, Suarez was able to score that spectacular winning goal. Korea played a great game but that slice of luck went our way, not theirs this time – that's football. It was a very hard-fought victory that took a lot out of us.

'The team's solidity and cohesion really came to the fore late on and, without getting carried away, I think that is a great quality to have, whatever team you're up against.'

It was interesting to note that Tabarez spoke about the match having 'taken a lot out of his team'. They were on a high but exhausted and that might create a problem if they hadn't recovered sufficiently for the last-eight match – especially if it was going to be against one of the world's best teams. But once again, fortune favoured the braves of Uruguay – Luis and Co. avoided the big guns. Instead they would face Ghana, arguably the weakest team left in the tournament. They were the team all the big guns had wanted to face – but a team that would be no pushover. Ghana were the pride of African football at the time and boasted such class players as John Mensah, Sulley Muntari and Kevin-Prince Boateng. The spine of the team was strong – and so too was their character and talent. The Ghanaians were the last African team left in the tournament and they saw this match as their representing the African nation against the rest of the world. It meant everything to them and they would give every ounce of effort and blood to make it to the semis.

But the Uruguayans were just as committed and determined

to advance. They were proud to have made it so far and, now that they had the taste of success and were in sight of glory, Luis and his team-mates wanted more. 'It was the biggest moment of their careers – a World Cup quarter-final and just two games away from the final and the biggest match in world football,' one commentator said. 'For Luis Suarez, as proud a Uruguayan as you could find, it meant everything. He wanted to make the final and make his country proud of him; he wanted to go down in the history books as the man who won the World Cup for his country. You could sense how geed up Luis and the rest of the team were when the match began. No way were they taking the opposition lightly.'

The team had travelled to Johannesburg for the match at Soccer City and you could feel the tension and sense of excitement as their bus arrived at the stadium and they disembarked for their meeting with destiny. It was true that none of them would underestimate the Ghanaians but, by the same token, none of them expected to be exiting the competition at the end of the match either.

Yet it was the underdogs who seized the initiative during a nerve-ridden opening half, with Muntari putting them ahead just before the half-time whistle. It was a shock to the system for the South Americans and coach Tabarez was at his best in the dressing room, rallying his men and telling them all was far from lost. A goal from Luis, Forlan or Cavani and they would be right back in it, the coach said, although he stressed they could not be complacent; they mustn't leave themselves open at the back, as a two-goal deficit would be difficult to overcome.

His men listened carefully and carried out his orders during the second half, with Forlan equalising with a goal from a free kick ten minutes after the interval. It was all Uruguay now but they could not break down a dogged Ghana backline, with Suarez getting closest with a late header.

Into extra-time and still the deadlock remained but now it was the Africans who were coming closest to breaking it.

With just one minute remaining and a penalty shootout looming, Luis Suarez would now show the Mr Hyde side of his Jekyll-and-Hyde character. Dominic Adiyiah's header was on its way into the goal and would have put Ghana into the semis. But Luis now made history for all the wrong reasons in terms of sporting gestures – he stopped a certain goal by palming the ball away with his hand. Just as Diego Maradona had cheated England by scoring with his hand – the so-called 'Hand of God' – in 1986, now Suarez cheated the African side by stopping them from scoring.

It was an instinctive move and it did the job. Ghana hadn't scored; Uruguay were still in the tournament but now down to ten men, as Luis was sent off. Of course, Ghana still had the chance to seal that semi-final spot from the consequent penalty but Asamoah Gyan could only watch in despair as his spot-kick hit the bar and bounced away to safety.

It was now down to a penalty shootout and it would be Uruguay who safely negotiated the drama, winning 4–3 on penalties. It was cruel on the Africans, who would have won but for Luis's intervention with his hand. After the game, there were two schools of thought back: one that Suarez was a cheat, the other – back in Montevideo – that he was a hero; that he had sacrificed himself, with an inevitable ban, for the sake of his team, for the sake of his nation.

Far from being repentant, Luis seemed confident that he had done the right thing and said that 'the hand of God now belongs to me'. He added, 'Sometimes in training I play goalkeeper so it was worth it. There was no alternative but for me to do that and, when they missed the penalty, I thought, "It is a miracle and we are alive in the tournament." Now we are in the semi-finals, although I was very sad because no one likes to be sent off.

'The celebration afterwards was impressive but very quiet because nobody gave us a chance but, with courage, we move forward.'

His coach Tabarez was quick to defend his talisman:

Saying we cheated Ghana is too harsh a word to use. Yes, he stuck his hand out but it's not cheating. It was instinctive. When there is a handball in the penalty area, there is a red card and the player is thrown out of the game. The player instinctively reacted and was thrown out of the match and he can't play the next match. What else do you want? Is Suarez also to blame for Ghana missing the penalty? We try to be dignified and, if we lose a match, we look for the reasons for it. You shouldn't look to third parties.

This is football. There are consequences to that handball and he didn't know that Ghana was going to miss that penalty. I'm emotional. We didn't play well but we've gone through. It seems there's something forcing us on – it must be the strength and unity of these boys. We are very excited.

People who believe in destiny might explain it otherwise. But I don't have an explanation for what happened today. It really was a hard match, we didn't play well but we survived very difficult circumstances. We conceded a goal at the end of the first half and we had a penalty against us in the last second. Maybe we didn't play that well but we had the guts to do it.

Diego Forlan backed that verdict, even claiming that Luis should now be declared a hero. He said, 'Suarez this time, instead of scoring goals, he saved one. I think he saved the game. We suffered but now we will be among the four best sides in the world. There are no words for that.

'As for the shootout, we felt we were going to faint with each penalty. My penalty kick? I thought about changing the way of kicking it, but I shot normally. It was necessary to score and I just thought about that.'

Former Uruguay star Gus Poyet, who would go on to manage Brighton and Sunderland in England, added his voice to those backing Suarez. The ex-Chelsea and Tottenham midfielder told BBC Radio Five Live,

I was little bit disappointed with some people talking about cheating. I think that is absolute rubbish. That is taking one for the team. That is making something happen for the rest of their life. That is helping one country of 3.5 million people to get to the semi-final for the first time in so many years.

You are telling me the player had to let the ball go in? Is that football? I think you're missing something really important here. I think you call it cheating when you try to score a goal with the hand, to take advantage when the referee cannot see that. Everybody saw that. The referee saw that. He gave the red card to the player [Suarez]. The player [Gyan] had the chance to score the penalty and didn't.

But Ghana were distraught and, inevitably, very much believed that they had been cheated out of a semi-final spot. 'In the same situation, there is no chance the Ghana players would have used our hand,' claimed John Pantsil.

FIFA announced that Luis would miss the semi-final against Holland but that his ban would be just for the one match. He had got off lightly – as long as his team-mates managed to beat the Dutch, at least. If they failed, well, his World Cup would have ended with the Ghana match anyway.

And so it would transpire: the match against the Netherlands without Luis was simply a match too far for his Uruguayan team-mates. They crashed 3–2 and exited the competition despite a brave effort. Before the match, Luis had admitted he was sad at missing out on a World Cup semi but happy as he knew he had helped the team make it to that stage. As Forlan would say, 'Luis gave us another chance and we took it.'

But without Suárez they could not bridge the gap against the talented Dutch and their World Cup adventure ended with defeat in Cape Town. There were tears afterwards as the dejected Uruguay players left the pitch, their dreams in tatters. Luis was also feeling low but forgot his own disappointment to console his team-mates, who had battled for ninety minutes and lost, as they trooped disconsolately off the pitch after the final whistle.

Uruguay coach Tabarez refused to lie down and die, instead proclaiming how proud he was of his players and the effort they had put in throughout the tournament. He said,

That was a match worthy of the World Cup semi-finals. I'm proud of my players. We're disappointed but we've shown everyone who wrote us off beforehand that we're not very far off the top. We gave it our best shot but it wasn't quite enough. I'm still completely satisfied with my team.

They reacted well to going a goal down, they fought back and equalised and they battled right to the end. I can't ask for more than that, nor can the players and nor can our country. It's the right result and we accept it. If I had the option of choosing how to lose a match, it would be pretty close to what happened today.

They were honourable words from an honourable man.

And his midfield star, Alvaro Pereira, backed up those sentiments, while also pointing out that the country's involvement in the event was still not quite over: 'The main difference wasn't individual class, nor was it team spirit. The main difference was the timing of the Dutch goals. They scored their second right in the middle of our best spell. But I'm very proud to be part of this group because we've made history in South Africa. Am I satisfied? I can't tell you until after the last match. The difference between third and fourth place matters a lot.'

But the opposition for the third/fourth place match were arguably even better than the Dutch team the Uruguayans had just lost out to: they would be up against an ever-developing, talented Germany – Germany who had thrashed England 4–1 earlier in the event and who were vibrant, youthful and as determined as Uruguay to finish third rather than fourth.

Luis Suarez would be welcomed back into the team for the match but, once again, it proved a match too far for the Uruguayans. They went down 3–2, with Cavani and Forlan on the scoresheet and Sami Khedira knocking in the winner for the Germans. At one stage in the Port Elizabeth Stadium, the Uruguayans had been leading 2–1 but the Germans are always dogged and battled right to the end to turn the result around.

Afterwards Luis and the team paraded around the pitch, clapping their fans and thanking them for their support. 'They may have lost but they had done their country proud,' one pundit said. 'Luis was smiling and pumping his fist in the air as the fans applauded them back. The team had arrived as underdogs who it was thought would even struggle to get out of the group and left as heroes who had finished as the fourth-best team in the world.'

There was little doubt either that Luis Suarez had made his mark. He was both hero and villain in the tournament but he would head back to Amsterdam to play his club football with Ajax, with his reputation soaring as a man who could score goals in the heat of the biggest of tournaments. OK, he had cheated with that handball against Ghana but many other footballers would come out and admit that they would have done just the same if it meant that would keep their nation at the World Cup table. Uruguay would leave South Africa as the surprise package of the tournament and Luis as one of the players marked down as a future star. When he touched down in Montevideo with the team, he realised just how much of a star he had already become, as he was hailed with cheers and smiles for his handball 'sacrifice' in the quarter-final against Ghana and his devastating form in the latter stages of the tournament.

Things would never be the same again – after the 2010 World Cup Suarez was a recognisable name in football world-wide. Now he wasn't just on the brink of stardom, he was on the brink of superstardom. In the next chapter we'll examine Luis's international career outside of the 2010 World Cup, to learn how he worked his way to the top with Uruguay and how he led them to a magnificent triumph in the Copa America after that World Cup in South Africa.

CHAPTER NINE

NATIONAL SERVICE

Luis Suarez was twenty when first chosen to represent his country in a major event. It was 2007 and he was a proud member of the Uruguay squad as they headed off to Canada for the Under-20 World Cup tournament. These were the finals in which another starlet who would end up in the Premier League also took a bow and made a deep impression. Sergio Aguero would end up as the tournament's top scorer, his six goals firing Argentina to their sixth title. Aguero, who would become a real folk hero at Manchester City, was also voted the Best Player of the event.

Luis had been unable to take part in the qualifying stages of the Under-20 World Cup. By now he had moved from Nacional to Groningen in the Netherlands and the Dutch side had refused to allow him to play in the qualifiers, although they could not prevent him from participating in the finals in Canada.

Uruguay were drawn in what, on paper at least, looked a fairly comfortable group and one that should have seen them move into the next round with few problems. They would play their matches in the relatively cool climate of British Columbia, in Burnaby, a city just to the east of Vancouver. Group B also consisted of Spain, Zambia and Jordan. While Spain, of course, would present a considerable obstacle to winning the group – their team boasted future stars who would go on to win the 2010 World Cup and Euro 2012 – Luis and Co. should have cruised home against Zambia and Jordan.

Of course, with Luis, few things in football are ever straightforward. He may have been playing up front with his future international colleague Edinson Cavani but he and the team struggled to make it out of the group. It all began brightly as they held the Spanish to a 2–2 draw in their first match. Indeed, Uruguay swept into a 2–0 lead with goals from Cavani and Suarez. Luis was a double hero – as well as scoring, he set up Cavani for his goal.

But Spain, with Gerard Pique and Juan Mata in their ranks, pulled the match back to 2–2, their final equaliser coming three minutes into time added on from Diego Capel. FIFA's official website summed up the situation best after what had turned out as a demoralising draw for Uruguay: 'The draw will feel more like a victory for Spain, who now face Zambia in Burnaby on 4 July. At the same venue, Uruguay must pick themselves up from this disappointing draw as they take on Jordan.'

There was much truth in that assertion: after looking as if they had got off to a flier by beating the much-fancied Spanish,

Uruguay had been pegged back and were demoralised. Rather than view the draw as a point gained, they saw it as two points lost.

Luis admitted as much after the match. He said, 'It was bad because we came so close to winning it. Over the course of the game, Uruguay had more goal-scoring chances. However, we're still in there fighting for a place in the last sixteen.' He added that he was happy with his own display and work rate. 'Yes, I'm happy to have scored my first goal at a World Cup. It was a beautiful goal. We sat back a bit after our goals and I also think tiredness played a part. We were very isolated up front and weren't really able to hold up the ball. That's something we need to work on.'

It was fighting talk but the truth of it was that the Uruguayans DID suffer something of an emotional hangover as they prepared for the next match. Luckily, they still managed to stumble through against Jordan, triumphing 1–0 with another goal from the prolific Cavani.

And so to their last group game – and a draw against Zambia would have been enough to see them through to the next round. Uruguay coach Gustavo Ferrin said, 'My players are improving by the game. Against Spain they dealt well with the pressure of kicking off their campaign against such a powerful side. I'm sure we'll play better against Zambia than we did against Jordan. We were lacking some competitive matches but now we're finding our rhythm.'

But Zambia's star midfielder, Clifford Mulenga, sounded a warning, saying that his team were now hitting form and that they fully expected to beat Uruguay. It may have sounded an idle boast but Mulenga appeared deadly serious when he said, 'I'm convinced we'll beat Uruguay. We're working hard to be more ruthless with the goal-scoring chances we create. Uruguay are a very good side but, as I see it, they're a team we can beat.'

Luis Suarez certainly didn't appear to have entertained any such thoughts, though. He was totally confident the South Americans would progress. Before the match, he said, 'We're confident we can go a long way. The team is very strong mentally and I know that, bit by bit, we're going to achieve great things.' But he was wrong: the Zambians, who had lost to Spain and drawn with Jordan, overpowered Luis and his team-mates. It would go down as the shock of the opening group stages, as Zambia won 2–0. They were helped by the sending off in the nineteenth minute of Uruguay keeper Mauro Goicoechea for a foul in the box on Emmanuel Mayuka.

From starting the match with the aim of pipping Spain for top spot in the group, Suarez flopped down on the pitch after the defeat, demoralised and fully aware that Uruguay had finished outside the top two, meaning a possible early exit and flight home with their tails between their legs. Mulenga, who had warned them that Zambia meant business, had scored the first goal and played a key role in driving his team forward and giving them the belief that they could not only match the Uruguayans but beat them too.

Of course, it hadn't helped losing their goalkeeper to a red card. As coach Ferrin said afterwards, 'When he was sent off, that changed everything for us. I make no excuses because they played well and are a good team but in that moment we lost not only our goalkeeper and a player but the structure of the match changed as well. I agreed with the decision and we tried to make adjustments but it was the key event for us. I think the situation also made the players disappointed. They could have reacted better.'

Fortunately for Luis, the early flight home would not be needed: Uruguay had managed to scramble into the round of sixteens as one of the best third-place teams. But they were not kidding themselves: they knew they would have to improve dramatically if they were to stay around even longer in Canada – especially as they would now come up against the United States, who had proved to be the surprise package of the tournament.

The Americans had topped Group D – a tough-looking group that also contained Brazil, Poland and South Korea. They had crushed the Poles 6–1 and beaten Brazil 2–1. It meant they were high on confidence as they prepared to meet Luis and Co. in Toronto.

In a match that went one way, then the other, the Uruguayans would far from disgrace themselves. Their twenty shots on target to the Americans' eight showed which team was the most offensive, as did their eleven corners to their rivals' six. But statistics themselves do not win games and it would be the Americans who would progress to the next stage, much to the anguish of Luis Suarez, who had set his heart on reaching the final and lifting the trophy.

Luis had fired his team ahead with less than twenty minutes remaining but the Americans dragged themselves back into the match and forced an own goal from Mathias Cardaccio with just three minutes left. That took the game into extra-time and now the Americans' superior strength and stamina took over and Michael Bradley was on hand to hammer home the winner in the 107th minute.

At the end of the match tempers boiled over as Uruguay allowed their discontent to surface – players from both sides had to be pulled apart by their coaches and officials. For once, Luis was not at the centre of the controversy. He stayed outside the brawl, watching with bemusement from a distance and then headed down the tunnel alone to the dressing room. He was too distraught and downbeaten; all his energy had been taken up in the battle to win on the pitch. He had given his all. Uruguay coach, Gustavo Ferrin, did not appear for the traditional post-match press conference – instead he kept his players in the dressing-room for half an hour so that they could 'cool down'.

It meant the USA would now advance into the quarter-finals and a match with Austria, while Luis and his team-mates would return to their hotel, collect their belongings and head home with their heads bowed. It was left to USA coach Tom Rongen to have the last word. He said,

We knew this was going to be a hard game. Uruguay was the toughest third-place finisher we could have faced. They're a high-quality team with many dangerous players and ways to hurt you. It was a hard-fought game, which went all the way down to the wire. Our regular keeper Chris Seitz couldn't play today after a collision in the game against Brazil but his understudy Perk came in and did the job for us. We haven't had too many tough games like this so far – hard, physical battles. But we stayed strong and showed them that we could mix it up too. We showed great heart today.

It was the end of Luis's first major competition for his country. He had learned much about tournament football and about being away from home for weeks at a time. And he would put that knowledge and experience – and the anguish of ultimate defeat – to good use the next time round.

Rewinding five months, Luis had won his first cap for the Uruguay senior team in February 2007. Naturally, he didn't arrive quietly on the scene, not simply staying in the background like any other awestruck youngster might. He had just celebrated his twentieth birthday and was enjoying life in the Netherlands with his new club, Groningen. Now he was determined to make a name for himself on the international scene – and he did just that, although probably not in the way he would have hoped!

Luis made his senior debut for Uruguay on 8 February 2007 in a 3–1 win against Colombia. But he was sent off in the eighty-fifth-minute after receiving a second yellow card for dissent. He had played well and made some useful contributions, so it was a blow when he was shown the red card in the friendly match.

But Luis was more concerned that he had let down his coach, Oscar Tabarez, who had gambled on him to start. The player admitted, 'It had been a dream of mine since childhood to play for my country and I was very grateful to the coach for giving me my chance. I simply cannot thank the players enough for how well they treated me.'

Tabarez would later tell him not to worry; that, OK, he shouldn't have been arguing with the referee but it had only been a friendly match and he wouldn't hold it against him in the future. He would wipe the slate clean and select him again. He also explained to Luis that he regarded him as one of his best prospects and believed he had a wonderful international career in front of him.

It was all that Luis had hoped to hear. Tabarez had made an important decision – he had recognised in Luis someone who needed encouragement; someone who responded better with an arm around the shoulder than with the big stick. It was a masterful move: Luis would now repay his coach with loyalty and a series of fine displays for his country.

And when later asked about that debut sending-off, Luis would even manage a smile and a wink and say, 'Yes... it was a bad start. But there were just a few minutes left and the coach said he understood what happened. It wasn't a big deal – and it was still a good debut overall!'

It was good that he could smile and laugh it off. But Luis also knew that Tabarez would not be as accommodating or forgiving if he let him down again. His aim now was to become an international player of repute and he wouldn't do that if he was constantly sidelined through suspension.

Luis started to repay that debt to Tavarez with his performances in the 2010 World Cup – as we have noted in the previous chapter – and really made his country proud of him the following year when he played a major role in helping to lift the Copa America. It was the nation's fifteenth triumph in the tournament and was especially sweet, as they lifted the trophy on the soil of one of their most bitter South American rivals, Argentina.

It was a well-earned reward for Tabarez, who had taken over at the helm when Uruguay were massive underachievers in 2006, and Suarez, who had been so determined to repay the coach's faith in him as an international player. At the end of the tournament Luis was voted its best player, much to his delight. The event's official website summed up his efforts in this way: 'Striker Luis Suarez, Uruguay, was voted the Best Player of the 2011 Copa America. With four goals scored and a lot of energy on the field, he led the experienced Uruguayan side... and Uruguay confirmed the hegemony in the competition.

'Against Peru in the semi-finals, Suarez scored twice to secure victory, ensuring a place in the grand final of the Copa America. The star of Liverpool was voted the Best Player, receiving 31.7 per cent of the votes from Internet users and journalists.' Luis was in coveted company to have won the award, as previous winners included the brilliant Brazilians Ronaldo and Rivaldo.

Uruguay had been pitched in Group C of the three groups at the start of the tournament, with Chile, Peru and Mexico. They progressed into the next stage by finishing runners-up to the Chileans. Luis had earned them a draw in their first match against Peru after the Peruvians had taken an early lead. They also drew their second match 1–1, this time against the Chileans, but won the third and final group game 1–0 against Mexico.

That set up a tough-looking quarter-final match with Argentina.

Uruguay drew first blood with Diego Perez scoring after just five minutes but Gonzalo Higuain levelled twelve minutes later. When Perez was sent off just after the interval, it looked grim for Suarez and his team-mates. But they had grown in fortitude in the years since Tavarez took over and refused to lie down, despite their hosts' clear superiority.

Three minutes from time Javier Mascherano was also sent off to even up the numbers and Uruguay held on as the match moved into extra time. Still stalemate prevailed and so the teams were thrown on to the mercy of the dreaded penalty shootout.

Uruguay scored from all their five penalties – with Luis second up – and goalkeeper Fernando Muslera became the hero of the hour as he saved Carlos Tevez's spot-kick. Afterwards, Lazio keeper Muslera said, 'We are very, very happy to make such a big step in the tournament. I hope I have just played one of the best matches in my short career. I'm very happy for all the people in Uruguay. This team deserves this win. We were better than Argentina, even playing with ten men. Then penalties are just a matter of luck.'

Defender Diego Lugano added, 'We fought more than we played. There is a long way to go yet. We have not achieved anything but we defeated the most difficult rival.'

And Luis said, 'I am just so happy and relieved that we have done it. It was hard and we played with ten men for a long time. But we dug in and we deserve our win. Now I hope we can go on to the final and win the cup.'

To do that, they would have to overcome Peru in the semis. This time they wouldn't need to dig in with ten men, or need a penalty shootout. Luis led them into the final with a brilliant brace, establishing himself as one of the most feared strikers in the world.

He struck twice in three first-half minutes to destroy Peru's dream and send his country's fans delirious. After the game he said he had enjoyed the match because it had been one in which the team could attack, rather than worry about conceding as they had against Argentina after having a man sent off. Luis said, 'Today was a match in which we had to go out and attack, to play, and luckily it worked out well. The first half was tough because we knew Peru would be very defensive. We had to try to take advantage of some chance to score. The goal in the first few minutes was a big blow to Peru.

'I think that to play the final in Argentina is great. Now we have to enjoy the moment. The important thing is we reached the final, which was our objective.'

Tabarez had taken Luis off after his second goal because he didn't want to risk him for the final. He admitted that Luis was so important to the team that he had decided to play safe and save him for the all-important next game. He said, 'It is one thing with Suarez, it is another without him in the final. He is a great forward; an elite player among forwards in the world. He often determines the outcome, as he did today.'

And so to the 2011 Copa America final in Buenos Aires – and Luis Suarez's date with destiny. Now only Paraguay stood between him and his first international trophy and he would inspire his team-mates into an awesome display of attacking football, leaving the opposition devastated and defeated.

Luis opened the scoring on thirteen minutes and a brace from co-striker Diego Forlan killed off Paraguay. Later a smiling Luis said he was delighted but dismissed suggestions that he was the star man who had dragged his team through the tournament. 'We played as a group,' he said. 'I think when groups are united like this, everyone together and going for the same thing, you can get things done. The important thing was starting well. With two goals in the first half, I think it was very difficult for them to come back.'

Then, acknowledging the backing of the fans who had travelled from Uruguay, he added, 'We must be eternally grateful to the people who have been supporting us.'

Coach Tabarez was also beaming after his team's achievement and said, 'This is not the most important thing in the world but it is very important for the Uruguayans. It allows us to be united.'

Diego Forlan was just as made up with the result and, naturally, with his two goals, which helped lift the trophy. The ex-Manchester United striker had just made a record eighty-second appearance for Uruguay and those two goals meant he had equalled Hector Scarone's national record of thirty-one goals. It also meant he had kept pace with his father Pablo and grandfather Juan Carlos, who had been Copa America winners too.

Forlan said, 'My grandfather won it, my father won it and now I have won it. It is a pride for the family. Three generations of my family have won this tournament. The name Forlan will live on in the history of football. It was a complicated game but the team played well. The early goal from Luis helped to simplify things.'

Twelve months later Luis was aiming for more international glory but now the venue was London and the 2012 Olympic Games. If history was anything to go by, he would be on a high after the final. Uruguay had only twice before entered the event, in 1924 and 1928, but on both occasions had won the gold medal! In 1924 they had beaten Switzerland 3–0 in the final in Paris and four years later had won 2–1 against old foes Argentina in Amsterdam.

For London 2012, the team prepared with three friendly matches, winning two and drawing one. In the first one, they drew 0–0 with Egypt and in the second they beat Chile 6–4, with Luis grabbing a brilliant hat-trick. Then, in the final warm-up, they beat Panama 2–0.

So spirits were high as the squad arrived at their London base in July 2012 for the Olympics. They had the weight of history behind them and the warm-up results suggested that they would be one of the favourites for the event, along with the ever-fancied Spanish. The squads for the tournament had to be made up of players under twenty-three years old – although each nation was allowed to choose three over-age stars. Uruguay chose Luis, Cavani and midfielder Egidio Rios.

The team would be in Group A, along with the United Arab Emirates, Senegal and the hosts, Great Britain. And they would be coached by Oscar Tabarez – the man who had masterminded their march to the World Cup semis in 2010 and Copa America glory the following year. He showed his instinctive faith in Luis by naming him his captain for the event; an honour which meant a lot to the player. 'It was a real big moment for Luis,' a squad source told me at the time. 'Here he was in London, at the Olympics, representing his country and also leading them into action. Luis was a very proud man when he led the team out at Old Trafford for their first match. He had always dreamed of playing for his country in major events and leading them to glory and here he was, leading from the front. He was very excited and very humbled by Tabarez's gesture.'

There was a certain irony in Luis leading Uruguay out at Old Trafford for their first match of the Olympics on 26 July. The stadium was, after all, the home of his club side Liverpool's greatest, bitterest rivals, Manchester United. So it was little wonder that he emerged from the tunnel adjacent to the famed Stretford End to a chorus of boos. Luis simply smiled at his tormentors and walked proudly to the centre of the pitch for the pre-match ceremonies. He was still smiling at the end of the game after leading Uruguay to a 2–1 win over the United Arab Emirates. The Uruguayans had to come from behind against a surprisingly good UAE team. The *Telegraph*'s Henry Winter best summed up the nature of Luis's Olympics afternoon in Manchester, pointing out that, 'Most fans present were here to support Team GB against Senegal later on but they created an occasionally noisy atmosphere, certainly reminding Liverpool's Suarez that he has few friends at Old Trafford. Uruguay's captain was influential, leading the line determinedly while Edinson Cavani scavenged to the right. Suarez played a part in both of his team's goals, for

Gaston Ramirez's free kick and then for his old Ajax team-mate, Nicolas Lodeiro.'

Tabarez said he was not unduly worried by the result. He pointed out that his team rarely did well in the opening games of major tournaments, pointing to how they failed to win in the openers in the successful 2010 World Cup and 2011 Copa America events. He said, 'You could say that the first games are not my specialty. At least we won – everything else can be worked on and addressed. The win was vital and we secured it after a first half in which we were dominated by our rivals. We had a great twenty minutes in the second period where we controlled but afterwards we could not keep up the same pace.'

Luis was also philosophical about the result, telling a friend, 'It was a win and that's all that matters, even if we didn't play that well. We can build on the result and improve our play as the tournament goes on.'

So not a bad day at the office for Luis on his first official Olympics engagement but tougher tasks lay ahead. Next up would be Senegal at Wembley – and they would certainly be no pushovers. As a footballing nation Senegal had come on in leaps and bounds in the last two decades and were recognised as one of the major forces in the African game.

Luis again led the team out, this time to a more welcoming round of applause from the more neutral London crowd. But the outcome would be much less appetising for him as his team crashed to a shock 2–0 defeat with a brace from Moussa Konate after Senegal had to play with ten men for an hour when Abdoulaye Ba was sent off after thirty minutes. Luis had the chance of grabbing a consolation goal in injury time but even that was to be denied him as Senegal keeper Ousmane Mane saved from him when he was through on goal.

The defeat was galling, as it also meant Uruguay had lost their first game ever in their Olympic history, bringing an end to an eighty-eight-year unbeaten run. But more urgently, it meant Luis and his team-mates would now have to get a result against their British hosts in the final match of the group at Cardiff's Millennium Stadium. Meet defeat and they would be heading home; an early exit few would have predicted before the tournament began.

Luis was, again, roundly booed as he led the team out at Cardiff and also during the Uruguayan national anthem. He had previously allowed the abuse to go over his head but now he seemed angered by it, shaking his head in fury. It wouldn't get any easier during the match; he was booed every time he touched the ball and it appeared to affect his rhythm and play. It was not one of his best days on a football field and his misery was compounded when Daniel Sturridge scored the only goal of the match. Great Britain were through to the quarter-finals, Luis and Uruguay were out.

GB boss Stuart Pearce was pleased that his team had stifled Luis and Cavani to progress. He said, 'I think everyone was inspired today by Bradley Wiggins and our rowing gold but I have to say the women's team beating Brazil in their last match gave us a really big lift too. We are delighted to be out of the group. We always felt it was going to be a tough group but we deserved to win it and the team is getting stronger and stronger.'

Luis, of course, was far from happy and he had a bone to pick with the British fans who had tormented him throughout the match. He said, 'I think they jeer me and they boo me because they must be scared of facing a player like me. They fear me but that doesn't affect me. I'm hurt because we lost and are going home. We all had a dream and that was to win the gold medal here. I can take the abuse. I don't mind. But I think it was a total lack of respect from the crowd to boo when we were trying to sing our national anthem. Those things should not happen.'

He was backed by his compatriot and Liverpool FC team-mate, Sebastian Coates. The centre-half said, 'I'm tired of this situation with Luis. I think it has gone on too far and I don't like to see him being treated like this. I know the kind of person he is and I think the abuse he gets is very unfair. He knows all his team-mates and the whole country are fully behind him and I think fans over here should leave him alone.'

Suarez's golden dream may have disappeared on the Cardiff turf but he would soon face further challenges on the international stage. The next would see him heading off to arguably the world's most glamorous and romantic footballing nation. Yes, the 2013 Confederations Cup would be held in Brazil and Luis was determined to win the tournament to make up for the Olympics letdown – and to show that Uruguay's 2011 Copa America triumph was no one-off fluke.

But they would have to do it the hard way – their opening match was against the world champions, Spain, and Uruguay found themselves outclassed in Recife. Spain won 2–1 and Luis's only consolation was that he scored his country's consolation goal two minutes from time. To be fair, he was honest enough to admit that his team had been outclassed; that they had struggled to get the ball, let alone take the game to the Spanish. He said, 'It's very difficult to generate any kind of danger when you don't touch the ball. Spain are the best side in the world. They are a candidate to win the World Cup.'

That view was backed up by Tabarez, who said, 'It could have been catastrophic for us but we improved and our professional image was rescued.'

But things would improve for Luis – as, indeed, he expected they would. He told FIFA.com,

Even before the game we knew that Spain were a better side than us. They use the ball really well and it's really hard to get it off them. What's more, they've got players in midfield with a huge amount of quality and they're very effective up front. They were the favourites and at the end of the day the result wasn't a surprise. We lost against the world's best national team, but we know that the competition's only just starting.

I think that we left a positive impression and we never let our heads drop, even when the game looked beyond us. The matches we've got coming up are different, and we've got to win them to progress.

Which is exactly what they would now do. They beat Nigeria 2–1 and then chalked up an awe-inspiring 8–0 win over Tahiti to advance to the semi-finals. In that 8–0 slaughter, Luis would score twice to become his country's all-time top scorer with a total of thirty-five goals. He was delighted to have made history but also determined to shoot his country into the final. That would not be easy – the semi-final now paired them with the hosts, Brazil, a daunting prospect in any tournament but even more so in their own backyard.

The match would take place in Belo Horizonte but it would end in disappointment for Suarez as Brazil booked a place in the final with a 2–1 win. Goals from Fred and Paulinho sent Brazil through, with Cavani replying for Uruguay. Both Luis and his coach declared themselves 'proud' after their run to the semis; naturally, they were downcast at not making the final but theirs was no disgrace. They had recovered from that opening defeat at the hands of Spain to leave their mark on the tournament. And in Luis's last three 'proper' tournaments – excluding the Olympics, which was largely made up of players under the age of twenty-three – he had twice been a runner-up (in the World Cup and here in Brazil) and a winner too (in the Copa America).

Both Luis Suarez and Uruguay had come of age on the international stage and he was looking forward to extending his impressive run with Uruguay in top international events. The World Cup in Brazil was a stage that was made for Suarez to show just what he had become: arguably the best striker in world football.

Now let's turn the spotlight back on Luis's exploits at club level – at the start of the Brendan Rodgers era at Liverpool.

CHAPTER TEN

MEET THE NEW BOSS

Luis Suarez was one of the last Liverpool players to return to work after the summer break of 2012. It was the start of August when he joined the rest of the squad at Melwood – his late return being a consequence of his appearance for Uruguay in the London Olympics. Luis had captained his country at the Games (although it had hardly been a success as they crashed out in the first round and he failed to hit the back of the net) and he had managed to fit in a brief holiday, back home in Montevideo.

By August he was fit and eager to impress as he joined the other Liverpool players for training at Melwood. His determination stemmed from him missing a chunk of the previous campaign because of the ban he had received over the Evra race incident – he felt he owed the team and the fans something after having to sit out all those matches.

There was also the little matter of having a new boss to impress. Dalglish had gone and in his place had come Brendan Rodgers, a softly-spoken Northern Irishman who had left his post at Swansea City to take over at Anfield. Rodgers was young (just thirty-nine), ambitious and keen to prove he had what it took to succeed at one of the giants of British football as well as at the likes of Swansea. He had certainly made a name for himself in South Wales, guiding the team to an impressive debut season in the Premier League (in which they finished eleventh) and showing Liverpool his worth with a 1–0 victory over them in the final league game of the season.

He swayed Liverpool's owners with an impressive interview and outline of where he expected to take the club and how he would do it. Attacking, attractive football had been his trademark at Swansea and he stressed at interview how he would employ the same formula at Anfield. He also made it clear that he well understood the importance of getting Liverpool back into the Champions League. Unlike Dalglish, he would prefer a fourth-place finish in the Premier League to a day out at Wembley – and that was just what Liverpool's American owners wanted to hear.

The esteem within which he had been held at Swansea was apparent when the club demanded – and received – in the region of £4 million from Liverpool in compensation for the loss of his services. On the last day of May 2012 Swansea chairman Huw Jenkins revealed that Rodgers was keen on the post. Jenkins said,

I was contacted by Liverpool last night and they expressed their wish to speak to Brendan regarding their vacancy. I had a discussion with Brendan to talk about their interest and his views on whether he wanted to speak to Liverpool. He expressed his wish with me to do that and he has spoken to Liverpool today.

Following on from discussions with Liverpool's owners, Brendan has informed us that he would like to take up their offer to manage Liverpool. At the moment we are currently in talks with the owners to agree compensation. We are trying to finalise that within the next twenty-four hours.

Twenty-four hours later, Rodgers would be gone from South Wales. He was revealed as the new man in command at Anfield on 1 June and admitted he would be sad to leave Swansea but that opportunities like the Liverpool job were just too big to ignore.

I have always been up front and honest. I have always said that I wouldn't be here forever and that one day I would go but I honestly never thought the opportunity would come round now. In my life and in my football, I have been very happy in Swansea but, when an opportunity to work at a club which is more than a club comes round, it's a professional challenge which is too good to turn down.

Liverpool are one of the dynasties of the game. They have won five European Cups and their status is up there with AC Milan, Inter Milan, Barcelona, Real Madrid and Bayern Munich. I turned them down once out of respect because I didn't want to go into a process and disrespect anything about Swansea. When they come in a second time and make you their number one target, then you have to think. We have seen over a number of years that the number of British coaches who get a chance at the big clubs is very few. When those opportunities come, and they may come only once, you have got to make a decision.

One of the biggest names in world football stepped forward to endorse Rodgers as the right man for the Liverpool job. Jose Mourinho, then manager of Real Madrid, had employed Rodgers in his backroom staff in his first spell as manager of Chelsea. Mourinho told the *Sun*, 'I am very happy with his appointment, especially because he did it as a consequence of all his amazing work at Swansea. Brendan is a good man, a family guy and a friend. When he joined us at Chelsea he was a young coach with lots of desire to learn. But he was also a coach with ideas, who was ready not just to listen but also to communicate and share.'

And one of Rodgers' first moves when he arrived at Liverpool in July 2012 was to seek out Suarez and tell him how important he viewed him to the team's success and how he planned to build the team around him and Steven Gerrard. Rodgers knew that the success of his first season depended largely on the two men – the club's two best players – backing him. He had plans to change the way the team played; to adopt a more flexible, less rigid, more exciting brand of football than under the previous regime. But he knew that would take time: time to chop and change the personnel and to instill his ideas into the players.

The first season would be, primarily, one of consolidation with gradual change as players were sold and others brought in. But even consolidation would require big efforts from the likes of Suarez and Gerrard. So it was little wonder that he took both men aside to explain his vision and his ambition and how both could be realised. In one of his first public statements after taking over at Anfield, Rodgers would hail the 'fantastic' talents of Luis – but also warn those he saw as underachievers that they needed to shape up or ship out. 'The focus was on the future and what I believe he can bring to the team in the way that we play,' Rodgers told Sky Sports News of his conversation with Suarez. 'He was fantastic, he was very open. You can only sell the dream going forward. There's a lot of nostalgia surrounding this club but it's important that we recognise this is 2012 and we're not in the Champions League. The top players want to play at that level. Steven Gerrard wants to play at that level, Jamie Carragher – they're players who have won it. In the coming years we'll strive towards that. If that's not enough for a player, then they will go – simple as that.'

Luis was impressed by Rodgers and his plans. So much so that he signed a new long-term deal with Liverpool after his return to training that August.

Suarez told Liverpoolfc.com,

To sign a new contract with Liverpool is unbelievable for me because I am so happy here at both the club and also in the city. That is important for me and I am very happy with my new contract. When you are a kid, everybody wants to play for Liverpool. I am here now and it is a dream for me, and now I am a Liverpool fan. I am happy off the pitch because the people of Liverpool are good with me and my family. I try my best on the pitch and when you are happy off the pitch, you are happy on the pitch. I want to say thank you to the fans because they are our 12th player. The supporters of Liverpool are unbelievable. Five or six years ago I watched on TV the stadium and the club, and now I play here and the supporters have helped me. That's very important for me.

The boss was just as delighted that his star man had committed himself to the club. Rodgers said,

When you have the opportunity to work with world-class players, it's fantastic. There were certainly a few clubs who were interested in him but over the off-season he and I communicated well – and he's committed himself for the long term here now. He's really looking forward to playing in this way of working. As a manager and for the supporters, I'm delighted because I know how important he is for them.

He's a winner. He wants to win. This is a guy who, whether it's raining or there's sunshine or snow or hail, he's out on the field. You very rarely see him in a treatment room. He loves his football and football is his life. It's his passion and I can relate to people like that; people who want to succeed and people who are passionate about success.

It was reported that Luis had signed a four-year contract that would see his wages tripled from a relatively modest (in footballing terms at least) £40k a week to £120k a week and put him on a par with the club's top earner, Gerrard. Rodgers clearly saw the importance of the little Uruguayan to his plans and was happy to endorse the deal with the club's money men. On Luis's part, it showed his commitment to the club and the fans he adored – he could quite easily have earned even more money and played in the Champions League immediately had he joined the likes of moneybag clubs such as Paris Saint-Germain. But he had proved his loyalty by staying at Anfield. 'Training is going fine. It has been a long time since I'd last seen the boys and the people who work at Melwood, so it's been great to do that in the last few days,' Luis would say at a subsequent press conference. 'I am happy because I have come back and I am training for the start of the next match. I am fit and I can play but it's not my decision – you'll have to ask the manager.' Of Rodgers, he added,

He is a good person. I spoke with him last week and he spoke fantastic to me. We know what he wants – he wants us to play with the ball all of the time and it's very important. We try our best in training and we hope to do so in the matches also. He tells us he wants

70-minute or 90-minute concentration all of the time in training. This is very important. I am enjoying training and happy with it. It's important for players to play with the ball all of the time – and with the manager that's what we're trying. I think he is a good manager and I was impressed with the work he did with Swansea last season. We played them twice and they tried to take the ball from us in good positions with lots of pressure. I think Brendan will try the same with Liverpool and we will all try to do our best.

Rodgers would reintegrate Luis slowly but surely back into the Liverpool team so that his star player would not pick up any niggling injuries after only just returning to training. The rest of the team had had a good couple of weeks' start on him and Luis would need time to reach peak fitness after missing out on a full pre-season. Yet by the end of September, he had scored his first goal of the 2012–13 campaign – and grabbed a hat-trick!

Suarez's first goal came in the home match against the reigning Premier League champions, Manchester City. Liverpool were still looking for their first league win under Rodgers and Luis appeared to have provided that when he struck just after the hour mark. The Uruguayan had scored with a fine free kick to put the hosts 2–1 ahead after Martin Skrtel had made it 1–0, only for Yaya Toure to equalise. Liverpool seemed energised, with Luis causing all sorts of problems for the visiting defence.

But Rodgers – and Luis – would have to wait for that first

Premier League victory of the season, when Skrtel turned from hero to villain with a dreadful back pass that Carlos Tevez capitalised on to make it 2–2 and give City a point they barely deserved. Rodgers admitted he was impressed by Luis and his goal and showed a commendable loyalty to his players and refused to blame the Slovakian defender for his side's failure to win. 'It's all part of the journey. I commend his courage to get on the ball. The easy thing is to smash it up the pitch. There is no blame here. Martin is a strong character and the other players and staff rallied around him,' Rodgers said.

The Suarez hat-trick came when he scored three times at Norwich for the second consecutive season. The Reds romped to a 5–3 win, with Luis hitting the back of the net on five, thirty-eight and fifty-seven minutes. It had taken its time coming but the win also marked Rodgers' first victory in the league as Liverpool boss. But just as importantly for the new boss, it marked the start of the impressive way he wanted the team to play – with powerful, fast, exciting, attacking football and with young winger Raheem Sterling also playing a key role.

Andy Carroll, the man brought in by Dalglish to partner Suarez up front, had departed Liverpool a month earlier after Rodgers decided he was not part of his thinking. My personal opinion was that Rodgers should have given Carroll more of a chance – a full season at least. From what I had seen of Carroll, he was much more than a typical bull of a centre-forward. He had good close control on the ground and was skilful with the ball at his feet. But Rodgers decided to dispense with his talents – without replacing him.

It was a gamble that would leave Liverpool striker-light by the Christmas of 2012 but few would argue that Rodgers got it wrong when he had the initiative to eventually bring in the wonderfully gifted Daniel Sturridge as Carroll's replacement.

Carroll joined West Ham on a season-long loan, with a permanent transfer to follow and a fee said to be around £18 million. The big Geordie was sad to be leaving Anfield, where he had struck up a good relationship with many fans, but said, 'I want to be playing games and obviously hoping to score some goals. I know the manager at West Ham [Sam Allardyce] well and some of the lads, so it is nice for me to come to a place where I know people. I'm hoping to add a lot of goals and create a few chances. I know Sam from Newcastle and he was a massive reason for me coming. When I worked with him at Newcastle it was great so it was a no-brainer really.'

Allardyce was delighted to get Andy and was quick to point out that he was more than just a big target man. He said, 'I think for all parties this is a great signing. Andy is an all-round footballer, but because he is 6ft 3in and one of his strengths is his aerial power, everybody dismisses the ability he possesses on the floor. Hopefully he can score goals for us and we will be in a very good position at the end of the year in the Barclays Premier League.'

Rodgers' attitude to the player was clear when he used the words 'Big Andy'. He said of the transfer, 'It is very simple: the club made a monumental investment in Big Andy and at this moment in time he's not playing. He made it clear from when we first met in the summer that he wants to play games and this is the last chance for him to go and do that.'

As I say, Rodgers would ultimately be vindicated in the following transfer window when he signed Sturridge for a fee that was undisclosed but was said by sources to be close to the £12 million mark. Carroll would eventually command a fee of £17 million, which meant Brendan had signed Sturridge and kept £5 million in the kitty. Not a bad deal by anyone's standards, especially as Sturridge proved what a great striker he was under Rodgers's guidance. Sturridge had always threatened greatness – under Rodgers at Liverpool he would finally deliver the goods.

But at the back end of September 2012 it would be Luis Suarez who would be winning all the plaudits as he scored that wonderful hat-trick at Norwich, with no strike partner to ease the pressure off his shoulders. 'His goals here were incredible last year and this was another masterclass in finishing,' Rodgers said after the win. 'His first goal was terrific. The second one typifies him because he missed his easiest chance he had but he didn't get disappointed, won back the ball, nutmegged the defender with an incredible piece of skill and then to finish the way he did was brilliant.'

The Liverpool boss was adamant that Suarez should have been awarded a penalty when he was fouled by Leon Barnett. Rodgers said, 'It was a stonewall penalty. I feel for Suarez, I really do. Everyone in the ground knew it was a penalty. Today the young guy Barnett elbowed Luis in the head and gave him a wee nudge just to make sure but the ref still didn't give it. If Luis is a player who goes down too easily, he would have done so in the second half when a defender caught him just before the fourth goal. Maybe one day we will get the decision. Until that point we just continue to concentrate on our performance.'

Even Brendan's Norwich counterpart Chris Hughton was impressed by the lethal finishing of Suarez, although, understandably, disappointed by the work of his defenders. He said of Suarez, 'You cannot afford to give him the opportunities we did and that is disappointing.'

And by the middle of November Luis was really hitting top form as he bagged a brace against Wigan, with Liverpool cruising to a 3–0 victory. The *Daily Mail* summed up the importance of Suarez to Liverpool now, saying, 'After a win like this, it is difficult to put a figure on Luis Suarez's value to Liverpool, but it stands somewhere between an enormous amount and priceless. Not that the Uruguayan is for sale, whatever reports of Roberto Mancini's interest at Manchester City claim. Two more goals taken with clinical efficiency took the twenty-five-year-old forward's Premier League tally for the season to ten. The rest of Liverpool's squad have scored six league goals between them.'

Certainly, Brendan Rodgers was now under no illusions as to how important Suarez was to his own future. He said, 'Luis is a master marksman, absolutely outstanding. He thrives on the pressure – he took his goals well and his movement was outstanding.' Even the then Wigan boss Roberto Martinez praised Suarez's showing, adding, 'It's the sign of a top player when you get half a chance and score a goal.'

But controversy never remained far from Luis – as the goals continued to amass, so too did the incidents concerning his character and integrity. In January 2013 he helped Liverpool to a 2–1 over non-league Mansfield in the third round of the FA Cup but was criticised for handling the ball before he scored the winning goal. Luis was seen clearly controlling the ball with his hand before guiding it into the net with his right foot. That prompted Stags keeper Alan Marriott to complain afterwards, 'When you see Luis Suarez laughing as he kicks the ball across the line... he knows himself what happened. Even Stewart Downing said to us that he couldn't believe professional officials missed that. When it turns out to be the decisive goal, it's a sickener for everyone.'

And Mansfield boss Paul Cox added, 'I don't want to be too hard on him because he's a fantastic player and it was instinctive but look at the reaction of all the other players. Ours all ran to the referee shouting handball while Suarez blasts the ball into the net in a way that says, "Yeah, I handled it and the ref's going to rule it out." I'm a little bit gutted because I think we warranted something out of the second half.' But Cox would later concede that he would not have complained if one of his own players had grabbed the winning goal in such a manner.

Mansfield Town chief executive Carolyn Radford was also critical, saying. 'I've absolutely enjoyed the day but I have to say it is a little bit like it's been stolen from us. Whether it's deliberate or not, I really do feel that it should be sorted out. We are a very good side and we put up a sterling effort. We are very proud of ourselves and it's very unfortunate that referees and officials can't pick up these things. It should be clarified and sorted out as soon as possible because obviously it wasn't in our favour and we should be going through to a replay at least.'

But Kop boss Rodgers had the last word, defending Luis as he said,

It's hit his hand but what do you want him to do in that situation? I don't think people would ask the question if it was anyone else. The ball has popped up, it's hit him and, after that, it is up to the officials what they do. I said to the fourth official straight away, 'Was that handball?' and he said they had seen it but they decided that it was not deliberate. It's not Luis's fault. But he has a thick skin and I think people are starting to recognise the ability the boy has. He is a brilliant talent as you have seen him in that little cameo when he has scored one and might have scored a number more. He is a wonderful professional and we need to appreciate him while he is here. He loves it. He is a great family man and a great player.

Liverpool FC believed that Luis Suarez was consistently getting unfair press because of incidents in his past that were constantly being dredged up in the present. In this case, it was indirectly being alleged that Luis was a cheat who would do anything to score a goal or win a match, with the implication that, well, hadn't he already been caught out doing that for Uruguay against Ghana in the 2010 World Cup? When he handled the ball to stop it flying in the net to save his country exiting the tournament – a move that would earn him a red card.

There was certainly some truth in the belief that certain elements of the media were 'out to get Luis'. In the Mansfield incident the referee and his assistants had taken the view that the player had handled the ball accidentally but some reporters jumped on the bandwagon regardless to put Luis down. They would not accept the official view from the officials because it was not as newsworthy – it did not create back-page headlines.

The press did not have to wait long for another fall from grace – and it would be a major one involving a totally unacceptable second biting incident – but, before that, Luis would continue to let his football do the talking. On 19 January 2013 he notched his seventh goal in three matches against Norwich, as Liverpool thrashed the Canaries 5–0 at Anfield in the Premier League. The match was also significant in that it was the first time the Uruguayan teamed up with his new strike partner, the aforementioned Daniel Sturridge.

He and Sturridge helped themselves to a goal apiece as Liverpool continued their domination of hapless Norwich. There were signs that Luis would forge a partnership with former Chelsea and Manchester City striker Sturridge – a partnership that Rodgers had decided would never pay off with the now exiled Andy Carroll. I was told that Luis believed he could play with Carroll in a Little & Large combo and that he also felt he could score goals from the many lay-offs the big man was capable of providing. But when Rodgers sent Carroll packing, Luis simply knuckled down and got on with his job.

Until January 2013, when Sturridge finally arrived from Chelsea, Luis had been forced for many games to forage alone for goals and pick up scraps provided by the Liverpool midfielders. But he was a professional and never moaned at the lack of a permanent strike partner. However, when Sturridge arrived, Luis was delighted: now he could really show off his talents if a strong partnership with the Englishman did develop.

And develop it would. The two would prove an ideal, modern-era combination as each made spaces and chances for each other, each working the channels to confuse defenders and cause mayhem. The partnership began against Norwich and, within twelve months, would be the most lethal one in British football – and, arguably, Europe as Suarez and Sturridge went on a goals spree.

Rodgers was beaming after the match when asked about the possibility of a prolific partnership between the duo. He nodded and smiled and said, 'Well, that wasn't bad for starters, was it?' And of Sturridge's cool strike for his goal – a simple tap-in at the far post – he added, 'That was the type of goal he was brought in for. He is terrific outside the box but he is a real killer in it. It's three goals in three games for him and I think there will be many to come. We have played well for most of the season but Daniel coming in adds that extra threat. He has pace and power and he has got a good touch and good skills.'

Sturridge would certainly prosper under Rodgers. He arrived at Anfield with the reputation of a player who had never realised his full potential and with claims ringing in his ears that he was too laid-back and not committed enough. He had played only twenty-one games for Manchester City in the three-year period of 2006–09, scoring five goals, and sixty-three times for Chelsea, notching thirteen goals from 2009 to his eventual transfer to Liverpool in January 2013. But he was never really given a chance at City or Chelsea – City were keen to bring in big-name stars to boost their profile under oil-rich owners and Chelsea mostly played Daniel out of position on the wing.

It was telling that, when he did play in his favoured central-striker role while on loan at Bolton from Chelsea in 2001, he scored eight goals in twelve appearances – a much more presentable goals-per-game ratio than at City or Chelsea. Brendan Rodgers had marked him out as a player who could adapt to his exciting brand of football when he took over as Liverpool boss but did not have enough time to thrash out a deal in the summer of 2012. He needed Andy Carroll off the books before he could even contemplate bringing in another big-money hitman and Carroll's move to West Ham only happened on the very last day of the summer transfer window. But Rodgers got his man in the winter window and was convinced that Sturridge would provide one of the missing pieces of the jigsaw he was putting together at Anfield. He believed Sturridge had the talent and intelligence to link with Suarez and that the duo could play together.

Sturridge also felt he could work with Luis and said he was happy to finally be putting down roots at a football club. Rodgers had told him he was in for the long haul and that suited Sturridge, as he had never really felt part of the furniture at City or Chelsea. Upon joining Liverpool, he told the club's website,

I am humbled and happy to be here. Brendan Rodgers said he sees me here for a long time and I also see myself here for a long time. I've not signed here to play for a couple of years and then move on. I've signed to be here for as long as possible. It's a humongous club – for me, one of the biggest in the world – and to have the fans and world-class players we have here is amazing.

And to have Luis Suarez as a team-mate is great. He's a very good player, very talented and rated as one of the best players in attacking positions in the world right now. It's good to be part of a team with him in and I'm sure we'll be able to play well together.

The partnership that would become known as Liverpool's SAS – Suarez and Sturridge – was born and it would become the cornerstone of Rodgers' new Liverpool as he plotted to get the club back into the Champions League.

Luis notched another first in January 2013 when he captained Liverpool for the first time in their FA Cup fourth-round clash at Oldham. He would say he felt honoured to be Liverpool skipper – following on from the days when he was captain at Ajax in Amsterdam – but would later add that it was a day he would rather forget in terms of the result: a shock 3–2 win for the Latics. Luis had made it 1–1 but could only shake his head in despair as the team he was leading failed to live up to the Liverpool FC name. He could only agree with his boss's assessment when Rodgers admitted, 'There is no excuse. Our application wasn't right.'

However, at the start of March Luis was smiling again as he racked up another hat-trick, this time against Wigan, in a marvellous 4–0 win at the DW Stadium, to take him on to twenty-one league goals in that season. It was a feat that would propel him into the record books as just the third Liverpool player to score twenty Premier League goals in one season, after Robbie Fowler and Fernando Torres. Luis left the field with the match ball tucked under his arm and the praise of his team-mate Stewart Downing ringing in his ears. The winger later said, 'He must be a nightmare for defenders. He can be quiet and then create something out of nothing.'

Rodgers was again generous in his praise for his number-one striker when he tried to quell talk that Luis might be unsettled if the club did not qualify for the Champions League: 'It's hard to say Champions League football isn't important,' he said. 'Top players want to play at the top level. But Luis has got a real affinity with the players, the supporters and the city. He genuinely sees there's a bright future for us. The next couple of years are important for us and for him.'

A week later, on 10 March, Luis chalked off another landmark in his Liverpool career with his fiftieth goal in all competitions for the club in the 3–2 home victory over Tottenham. He was also named Man of the Match. Luis had scored the first goal and was instrumental in the winner – a Steven Gerrard penalty awarded after Suarez was fouled in the box by Benoit Assou-Ekotto.

It looked as if Luis Suarez had finally turned the corner in his controversial football career. Already he was the hero of the Kop and his divine footballing talent was now being recognised throughout Britain. But then he went and put his foot in it again... or, to be more precise, his teeth. He was about to become embroiled in a second damaging biting incident to add to his rollercoaster exploits in European football.

CHAPTER ELEVEN

THE BITE

There had been many controversial incidents in Suarez's career – the bite ban in Amsterdam, the race bust-up with Evra and the subsequent row over Luis's refusal to shake hands with the Frenchman – but in April 2013 Suarez would hit a personal rock bottom during the 2–2 draw with Chelsea at Anfield. All the good work he had done with a series of brilliant performances and sporting gestures to fellow players was forgotten as Luis sunk his teeth into Blues defender Branislav Ivanovic's arm.

Even Liverpool fans on the Kop were shocked into silence by the totally unacceptable action by the man they adored.

And it was all the more shocking and unacceptable because Luis had done the same once before, back in Amsterdam. Surely, you thought, he would have learned from the fallout of that incident and done everything in his power to ensure it did not happen again. And I was told by sources that, yes, Luis had discussed the Amsterdam incident with friends and vowed never to repeat it but that sheer animalistic instinct had propelled him back into the fire with Ivanovic; that he had become manically frustrated – not even with the Serbian defender but with himself – after he gave away a penalty by handling the ball in the area. Luis admitted that he 'lost it' after the Blues went 2–1 ahead from the subsequent spot kick – that was when all his previous good work and good intentions flew right out of the window. The madness had descended and he was unable to see through it, let alone stop it in the seventy-third minute of the match.

Only when he had bitten Ivanovic did sanity seem to return as Luis staggered away, looking almost as traumatised as his victim, as Chelsea keeper Petr Cech remonstrated with him and asked if he realised what he had just done. But by then it was too late: the damage had been done and it would leave him a leper in English football and almost drive him out of Liverpool. It would only be the constant support of his manager, Brendan Rodgers, and the Liverpool fans that would keep him at the football club.

Luis immediately apologised for his 'inexcusable' behaviour but argued that he should not be banned for more than three games – the FA's usual punishment for 'violent behaviour'. An FA statement summed up the player's view, stating, 'Luis Suarez has accepted a charge of violent conduct, following an incident with Chelsea's Branislav Ivanovic in Sunday's fixture at Anfield. However, Suarez has denied the FA's claim that the standard punishment of three matches is clearly insufficient for this offence. The incident was not seen by the match officials and has therefore been retrospectively reviewed. An independent regulatory commission will hear the case tomorrow.'

Luis's plea for leniency was hardly helped when a spokesman for British Prime Minister David Cameron argued that he should be made a scapegoat.

'It is rightly a matter for the football authorities to consider,' the Prime Minister's spokesman said. 'As part of their consideration, I think it would be very understandable if they took into account the fact that high-profile players are often role models.'

Inevitably, the commission came down on the side of the FA. Luis was punished swiftly and hard with a ten-match ban, much to the dismay of Liverpool FC, who declared themselves 'shocked' by its severity. The three-man independent commission decided on the suspension after weighing up the FA's charge of violent conduct and Liverpool's written analysis.

The FA said, 'A three-person independent regulatory commission today upheld the FA's claim that a suspension of three matches was clearly insufficient and the player will serve a further seven first-team matches in addition to the standard three. The suspension begins with immediate effect.'

It meant the striker's season was over in April and that he would also miss the start of the following campaign. Liverpool would have to cope without him for the remaining four matches of the 2012–13 campaign and six of the following 2013–14 season. It was a massive blow for Suarez and Liverpool as the Anfield club's MD Liverpool managing director, Ian Ayre, admitted, 'Both the club and player are shocked and disappointed at the severity of today's Independent Regulatory Commission decision.'

Ayre had made it clear that the incident would not force Liverpool to sell the striker. He said,

It affects his future in the sense that we have to work with him on his discipline but Luis is a very important player to the club. He's a very popular player with his team-mates. As we keep saying, he signed a new four-year contract last summer and we'd all love to see him here throughout that contract. He's a fantastic player, top scorer and everything we'd want in a striker, so there's no change there. This is more about getting him back on the right track and it's largely down to Brendan now to work with him on that side of his character.

It was then revealed that Luis would not face a police charge over the incident. A spokesman for Merseyside police said, 'Merseyside police can confirm that following an incident at the Liverpool v Chelsea game officers have spoken to Branislav Ivanovic in person. He had no apparent physical injuries and did not wish to make a complaint. This is now a matter for the Football Association.'

At the time, Luis Suarez had fallen out of love with English football – and English football had certainly fallen out of love with him.

There was much talk that he would seek a move away from Anfield and Luis did little to end such chatter when he spoke about the incident for the first time in June 2014 on returning home to Montevideo. Suarez, speaking on Uruguayan national television, said, 'The incident with Ivanovic – I know I made a mistake, it was me, my fault and he did not do anything to me. I was angry because I had given away a penalty for hand ball. I was the cause of the penalty against my team – I saw red and completely lost it. I can't really explain it and I am so sorry. But still people can be very cruel and the reaction was amazing.'

Suarez added that, yes, he was contemplating leaving Liverpool and that he dreamed of joining Real Madrid. 'Of course, I would like to play with Cristiano Ronaldo – he is a great player. You never know but it is complicated. At the moment he is in Madrid and I am in Liverpool and I do not know what is going to happen.'

The TV interviewer then asked him if he and Ronaldo could outscore Barcelona's magic duo, Lionel Messi and Neymar. '[Laughs] I do not know – that is complicated! Barcelona have won so many trophies and Neymar will need to adapt because all eyes are going to be on him. And, as I say, Ronaldo is in Madrid and I am in Liverpool. I do not know yet what is going to happen.'

Ivanovic would refuse to comment on the biting issue in its immediate aftermath. It would be a month down the road before he finally broke his silence and admitted he hadn't been as concerned about it as everyone else seemed to be. He told Serbian newspaper *Vecernje Novosti*, 'When it happened I was really surprised and, of course, shocked. But when the match ended, it all cooled down. I almost forgot about everything. The next day we talked on the phone and I accepted his apology. I didn't attack him for what he'd done but I also didn't defend him. But I forgive him. For me, that can happen. But I really don't care too much.'

But Brendan Rodgers was unhappy with the decision and claimed the intervention of people like David Cameron had influenced the independent panel in their judgement. The Liverpool boss said, 'The Prime Minister even chipped in with something which was a different matter altogether. There's no doubt if you have those high-profile figures making those sort of statements, there will be a bias. That's the first time I've heard of an independent panel being dictated to by so many people.'

To which Cameron replied, 'I made my own views clear, just as a dad watching the game. I have a seven-year-old son who loves football, loves watching football and when players behave like this, it sets the most appalling example to young people in our country.'

Rodgers then added that he believed the FA had punished 'the man', rather than the offence.

But eventually, Suarez and Liverpool decided not to appeal against the ban and to draw a line under the unsavoury incident and, hopefully, to move on. Suarez said, 'I know that all the things that are happening to me in England will help me to improve my conduct on the field. Right now, I just want to focus on becoming a better footballer on and off the field.

'Many things have been said and written about me. I just tried to do my best on the field. I hope to come back early to play.'

And Rodgers agreed that the matter was closed and stressed

that Luis was 'still very much part of our family and our future'. No way did he want to lose his best player – and no way was he going to allow him to leave, however much the Uruguayan tried to do so.

The Liverpool supporters on the myriad Internet fan sites appeared torn over the issue: many believed Luis had been punished too harshly and were just relieved he was staying. But others felt the good name of the club had been dragged through the mud by the player. One fan summed up the latter case, saying, 'I'm a little disappointed at Brendan Rodgers. Initially he seemed to be saying that the reputation of Liverpool football club had to come first before any player. Now he has joined those carping at the length of Suarez ban and, by implication, offering excuses and sympathy. The dignity and reputation of the club is better upheld by accepting the judgment as the player has now done.'

Another supporter expressed the views of those backing Suarez, saying, 'I agree that biting is unacceptable. However, the player has shown true remorse for his action and has sincerely apologised to all. While I think the ban seems appropriate, I sincerely hope that, for the sake of the future of such a dedicated player, the ban can be confined to the rest of this season with a warning that if it happens again in the future, he could be banned indefinitely.'

The incident appeared finally to have run out of steam but Luis then made matters worse from May 2013 by continually telling anyone who would listen that he wanted to leave Liverpool. It was a poor show: the club and fans had stood loyally by him after his disgrace and his reward to them was to selfishly keep saying he wanted to quit. At the start of August he made his feelings known to the British media, saying,

Last year I had the opportunity to move to a big European club and I stayed on the understanding that, if we failed to qualify for the Champions League the following season, I'd be allowed to go. I gave absolutely everything last season but it was not enough to give us a top-four finish – now all I want is for Liverpool to honour our agreement. I have the club's word and we have the written contract and we are happy to take this to the Premier League for them to decide the case but I do not want it to come to that.

I don't feel betrayed but the club promised me something a year ago, just as I promised them that I would stay and try everything possible to get us into the Champions League. They gave me their word a year ago and now I want them to honour that. And it is not just something verbal with the coach but something that is written in the contract. I'm not going to another club to hurt Liverpool.

They defended me, just like I defended them on the pitch. The players have always supported me and I'm grateful for that. It's the same with the supporters. I don't think the supporters are angry – I think they understand a player when he has the ambition to triumph at the highest level. When you are at a club for as long as you are together, you stick up for each other but that does not give the club the right to go back on their commitment.

I'm 26. I need to be playing in the Champions League. I waited one year and no one can say that I did not give everything possible with my team-mates last season to get us there. It is not as if I am asking to move to a local rival. And I would not consider moving to a club outside the Champions League. I have made my desire to move known in private various times and now it feels like the time for me to make it public. I have to put my career first. People say Liverpool deserve more from me but I have scored 50 goals in less than 100 games and now they could double the money they paid for me.

Liverpool will always be special for me: my daughter was born here. I know I have made mistakes in my time here but I have apologised lots of times. This is not about that. This is about the club having agreed to something both verbally and in the contract which they are now not honouring. People may accuse me of showing a lack of loyalty but last season we told Liverpool there was interest from a top European club but they told me, 'We've got a new coach and we're going to push for the Champions League.' I spoke with Brendan Rodgers several times and he told me, 'Stay another season, and you have my word if we don't make it then I will personally make sure that you can leave.'

Liverpool is a club with a reputation for doing things the right way. I just want them to abide by the promises made last season.

The player believed he had a clause in his contract that would enable him to leave should any club offer more than £40 million for him. He now took his case to the Professional Footballers' Association, whose chairman, Gordon Taylor, admitted that the Uruguayan had asked for help in securing a move and who spoke about the contract clause. Taylor said,

These buy-out clauses have caused no end of problems in the past and they continue to do so because of the way they were drafted at the time. Luis believes the £40 million amount that is mentioned, if that is offered, that gives him the right to go. Liverpool, from their side, are saying that is a minimum figure from which they will consider negotiation and of course they will want to keep the player, unless they replace the player with someone as good or better, which is not going to be easy in a short period of time.

We have raised this issue with the Premier League that buy-out clauses should have a great deal more clarity because I've never seen one yet that hasn't caused trouble. It's also down to discussions Luis had with the manager as well and of course you have the owners involved. There are different ways it can be interpreted. If it goes to the Premier League, it will take time and the window is then closed. It is a delicate situation and we are trying to help. We have been asked to try and help to sort the situation out and we have been trying to do that. The lad has had a chequered past but he is also an extremely good footballer and this is about a situation on the interpretation of a contract. You want contracts to be straightforward and clear and on this issue it is not clear. It is open to different interpretation by lawyers so, at the end of the day, it is about if an agreement can be reached.

The situation was now further complicated when Arsenal tried to trigger the player's release for £40 million plus £1. It was rejected but caused a temporary rift between the clubs, with Liverpool again denying such a clause existed. Twelve months down the road Liverpool owner John W. Henry would admit that the clause DID exist but that they chose to ignore it as they did not want to sell Luis. Speaking in America, he told the press,

Luis Suarez is the top scorer in the English Premier League, which is arguably the top soccer league in the world. And he had a buy-out clause – I don't know what degree I should go into this – but he had a buy-out clause of £40 million: more than 60 million [US] dollars. So Arsenal, one of our prime rivals this year, they offered £40 million plus £1 for him and triggered his buy-out clause.

But what we've found over the years is that contracts don't seem to mean a lot in England – actually not in England, in world football. It doesn't matter how long a player's contract is, he can decide he's leaving. We sold Fernando Torres for £50 million. We didn't want to sell but we were forced to. For the first time [with Suarez] we took the position that we weren't selling. Since apparently these contracts don't seem to hold, we took the position we're just not selling and it's been great for Luis, it's been great for us, and what will happen at the end of year... I think we're going to make Champions League and we have a small chance of winning the Premier League this year. We have three gentlemen up front: Suarez, [Raheem] Sterling and [Daniel] Sturridge. Those three are young, and I think they could be together for a long time.

So Suarez had stayed because the Liverpool owner had decided to hold his ground; John W. Henry had decided not to be bullied by Arsenal or the player. Both Liverpool and Suarez would be grateful, as they went on a terrific run that would lead to Champions League football the following season. In the summer of 2013 Luis had been selfish, belligerent and out of order as he tried to engineer a transfer away from Liverpool. The club and the fans had shown him real loyalty after he was banned for the Ivanovic bite. Their reward was his disloyalty. He certainly owed them – and he would repay them the following season. By standing their ground and refusing to let him leave, John W. Henry, Brendan Rodgers and Liverpool FC would prove to be the making of Luis Suarez. And he, in return, would now lead them back to the promised land. The season 2013–14 would finally bring to an end the club's exile from the European Champions League as they finished in the top four of the Premier League. For Suarez, finally, there would be a happy ending after yet another controversy in a career littered with them. His unhappiest hour would prove to be the dark night before a bright new dawn.

Suarez had stopped running away: he was home at last. And home was Liverpool. Before we look at how Luis transformed a nightmare beginning to a dream ending for Liverpool in the 2013–14 season, let's cast an eye over how his genius and controversies in many ways mirror those of another foreigner who made the Premier League his kingdom almost twenty years earlier... and behind enemy lines.

CHAPTER TWELVE

FOREIGN LEGION

Of course, I'm well aware of the enmity between Liverpool and their bitterest rivals, 30-odd miles down the East Lancs Road. But it strikes me that if I had to compare the genius of Luis Suarez with any other Premier League player ever, it would probably be Eric Cantona. And I can understand why some members of the press pack have, indeed, labelled Luis as 'Liverpool's Cantona'. For, just as Cantona was United's catalyst to success when they had been starved of it in the 1990s, so Luis has been the spark for Liverpool's current resurgence. And, just as Cantona's genius was matched by his fiery temperament and rebellion, so Luis has trod a similar path of controversy and outrage with his actions on the football field.

In one of his most famous comments in 1996 – a year before he quit United – Cantona would say of his time in Manchester,

'I feel close to the rebelliousness and vigour of the youth here. Perhaps time will separate us, but nobody can deny that here, behind the windows of Manchester, there is an insane love of football, of celebration and of music.'

Certainly, Suarez is of the same opinion in Liverpool: he might have felt homesick at times but he had settled fairly well in the north-of-England city and forged a wonderful bond with the Liverpool fans.

But there were differences between the two men. While Luis's childhood was fractured and difficult in Montevideo, Eric was settled as a youngster and given the freedom by his parents to develop as a creative being.

Cantona was born on 24 May 1966 in Marseille in the south of France – his parents named him Eric Daniel Pierre – just two months before England's greatest footballing triumph, when Bobby Moore would lift the World Cup at Wembley.

His father's family originated from Sardinia, his mother's from Spain – that production line perhaps helping to explain the volatility of his mixed Latin temperament, similar to Luis's. Yet from an early age Eric was no 'brat'; indeed, he much preferred painting and reading in the cave high above the city of Marseille that the family called home.

His father Albert loved painting and hunting. By trade, he was a psychiatric nurse but he also loved to play football, earning a reputation as a fine amateur goalkeeper. Albert would tell Eric, 'There is nothing more simple than football. Look before you receive the ball and then give it and always remember that the ball goes quicker than you can carry it.'

Luis's father Rodolfo also enjoyed playing football and was

a good player but he walked out on Luis when he was young, leaving him without a male role model to look up to.

Eric's mother Eleonore faced a battle similar to Luis's mum Sandra – bringing up her children without much money.

The Cantonas were poor but Eric loved his young life, later claiming he was the 'son of rich people' because of the variety of cultural and artistic activities open to him with his family. By the age of five – like Luis – he was playing football in the streets and fell in love with the game, saying, 'You start wanting to play [it] when you are three, four or five... you know you have a passion when you can't stop playing the game, when you play it in the streets, in the playground, after school and when you spend your time at school swapping photographs of footballers... playing football in the streets gave us a tremendous need for freedom.'

And like Luis in Montevideo, Eric certainly had his run-ins, on and off the football pitch, while in his homeland. His career in France was littered by run-ins with authority and suspensions.

By the age of twenty-five he had quit France and joined Leeds United in February 1992, initially on a loan deal that would see the Yorkshire club pay Nimes £100,000 and Cantona's wages until the end of the season.

Similarly, Luis would quit his homeland for Ajax in Amsterdam and earn the reputation as a brilliant striker that would bring him to the attention of the world's biggest clubs, including Liverpool.

Luis would find his place at Liverpool, first with Kenny Dalglish and then Brendan Rodgers – managers who believed in him and put their faith in him – just as Cantona finally found his 'home' with Alex Ferguson.

Cantona would make an immediate impression on his new club, as would Luis. I am told by United insiders that Fergie 'knew immediately that he had struck gold' and that the signing of the Frenchman was the last piece in his jigsaw at the time. Ferguson would later comment on how Cantona had thrilled him by 'walking in as though he owned the bloody place' and that, while some players found Old Trafford and the United aura too much, Cantona was at the very head of the queue of those who 'simply belonged' from day one.

Similarly, Luis Suarez exuded a similar confidence at Liverpool. He was born to be King of the Kop.

Cantona arrived in Manchester in November 1992 and soon got to work, showing the kids in the team how it was done and bringing a huge confidence boost to the club. Fergie had joked that United could do with Superman to take them to the next level... well, he didn't get the man of Krypton but the next best thing: his very own footballing superman – just as Rodgers was confident Suarez would be for Liverpool as they gunned for the Premier League title in the 2013-14 season.

When Cantona arrived, it had been twenty-six long years since United had last won the league title – just as Liverpool had not won it for twenty-one years (1990) when Suarez joined them. Within six months of Eric's arrival, the wait that had lasted from 1967 was finally over.

And, when Rodgers took command at Anfield, he was confident that Luis would prove a similar catalyst for them.

But you take the bad with the good with footballing Gods like Suarez and Cantona. The Frenchman had picked up the tag 'Le Brat' for his adventures in his native France and had managed to fall out with Howard Wilkinson at Leeds within nine months of arriving in the UK.

But it was his very temperament that endeared him to Manchester United fans – indeed, most of us can relate to the rebel, usually we just do not have the guts, or if you look at it another way, the foolhardiness, to act like one.

Luis, like Cantona, certainly has that darker side: a side that led to suspensions from the game – disciplinary setbacks that would also hit both their clubs.

But, just as Ferguson stuck by Cantona after his kung-fu attack on a fan at Crystal Palace in 1995, so Rodgers would stand by his man Suarez after all hell broke loose when he bit Branislav Ivanovic.

Cantona was sent off at Palace, four minutes into the second half of United's Premiership match there – which ended 1–1 – for kicking out at defender Richard Shaw. As Eric made his way from the pitch, twenty-year-old Palace fan Simmons rushed down the stands to taunt him. Cantona was enraged and he responded with his kick and then exchanged punches with Simmons. As a result, he was banned from football for nine months.

Looking back on the incident, there is, of course, no defence for the fact that Cantona finally took his Bruce Lee obsession one kick too far. Sure, Simmons was out of order but verbal abuse happens all the time in football. I am assured by one Palace insider that Simmons, a self-employed glazier and 'victim' of Cantona's attack, was not the loyal fan of the club he was usually portrayed as. Indeed, I am told his 'first love' was not Palace but Fulham and that he returned to Craven Cottage after he was given a life ban from Selhurst for his part in the run-in with Cantona.

Simmons would claim that all he said to Cantona – in true Leslie-Phillips-stiff-upper-lip-style English – was along the lines of, 'Off, off, off! Go on, Cantona, that's an early bath for you.' Cantona would say it was a much more racist attack, along the lines of, 'Fuck off back to France, you French motherfucker'. Simmons remains adamant that Cantona lied: 'For God's sake, you can't say a worse thing about anyone [than what he alleges I said], can you? What he did in saying that was totally unjustified. The man is filth. How can he accuse me of saying such a thing? Where has this allegation against me come from? From him. It ruined my life. And that is why it is inexcusable.'

But standing by Cantona was arguably the defining moment of Ferguson's managerial career for, with the Frenchman on board, his team won trophy after trophy.

And Rodgers' determination to keep Suarez at Anfield after the Ivanovic bite was the decision that propelled Liverpool into the Champions League in 2014 as Suarez's goals took them into the top four of the Premier League. Ferguson never had the slightest doubt that he and United should move heaven and earth to keep the Frenchman, just as Rodgers remained convinced in his belief that Luis should be kept at Liverpool – not just because he would become good but because he would become one of the three best players in the world, along with Lionel Messi, Cristiano Ronaldo and, yes, better than Rooney!

The Liverpool boss put his reputation on the line for the mercurial Uruguayan and Suarez rewarded him with a series of outstanding displays in the 2013–14 season. There is also an argument that not only the managers but the two players have benefitted from the decisions to move mountains to keep them at their respective football clubs.

It appeared that Cantona would sign for Inter Milan after he was banned for the kung-fu kick, while Luis was receiving affectionate noises from the likes of Real Madrid during his ban for the Ivanovic bite.

In another era, Sir Matt Busby had struggled and ultimately failed to 'save' Georgie Best from himself but Fergie did save Cantona from imploding. If Eric had left United during the ban for Italy, who is to say what would have happened to his career?

Would he have knuckled down and changed in the San Siro? Would he suddenly have lost the edge that made him the player he was? More likely his indiscretion at Selhurst Park would have been followed by further speedy black marks at Inter and he might have been cast out of the game for good.

Similarly, if Suarez had gone to Madrid and split from his mentor Rodgers, his own career could have nosedived as he struggled without the Liverpool boss's obvious affection and guidance. Fergie saved Eric – and his own developing team – by showing him amazing love and loyalty. Brendan did the same with Luis when many pundits and fans were clamouring for him to be exiled to Spain. In Alex Ferguson, Eric finally found the only manager he had ever played under who would plead with him to remain a part of his football club. Again, a similar situation to that of Suarez and Rodgers.

Now let's turn the spotlight on the 2013–14 season and how Luis took Liverpool back into the Champions League with a wonderful season's work.

CHAPTER THIRTEEN

A LEAGUE OF
HIS OWN

For Luis, Brendan Rodgers and Liverpool, the 2013–14 season would get off to a tough start – but ended with them in dreamland. After the constant distractions of 'will he leave, won't he leave?' Luis finally accepted that he would have to stay because the club would not allow him to do otherwise. It was a victory for Brendan Rodgers and a victory for football – at last a club had stood up to a player and refused to cave in when he demanded to leave for what he viewed as pastures greener. On 14 August 2013 Luis conceded that he would be playing for Liverpool in the new season and even talked of signing an extension to his contract. Martin Charquero of GolTV Latino America said Luis had told him of his intentions and tweeted, 'Luis Suarez confirms to me he will not leave Liverpool. The support of the fans has influenced his decision. Suarez sees it as likely that he'll sign a renewal [extension] to the contract that binds him to Liverpool.'

At the same time, Liverpool skipper Steven Gerrard made it clear he wanted Suarez to stay and said he would do everything in his power to make that happen, 'It's very important that he stays. He is one of the best players in the world. I can understand why clubs are showing an interest in him. If I can use my influence to try to get him to stay, then of course I will because I love playing with him and I don't want him to go. For Liverpool to be successful and move forward we have to keep our best players.'

Two days later came the development that would delight Rodgers, Gerrard and Liverpool fans everywhere as Luis returned to training. The breakthrough that enabled his return was simple: he apologised to his manager and team-mates for his behaviour in trying to secure a transfer away from the club. That apology was enough for Rodgers to bring him back into the fold at the training sessions at Melwood. On Luis's return, his team-mate Jordan Henderson told Sky Sports, 'It is obviously a huge boost. He is a world-class player and you have got to try and keep your best players. We look forward to the new season and hopefully he can pick up from where he left off.'

Of course, there was still the small matter of Luis's ban – he still had six matches to serve as the season got underway. But his efforts in training and determination to prove his newfound loyalty to the club encouraged Rodgers to believe that the team would take off when he did return. Ironically, Luis would return against Liverpool's biggest rivals, Manchester

United – just as United bad-boy Eric Cantona would make his comeback against Liverpool after his ban in 1995 for that kung-fu kick on a Crystal Palace fan! It was yet another one of those uncanny similarities that Luis and Eric shared.

It was 25 September when Luis completed his ten-match suspension and finally pulled on the famous red shirt of Liverpool once again. He trotted out proudly at Old Trafford for his first appearance of the new campaign. His last competitive game for Liverpool had been at the back end of April, although he had played for Uruguay in two World Cup qualifiers and the Confederations Cup since then.

Before the United match, Luis's boss, Rodgers, told a press conference that his number-one striker was 'champing at the bit' to return and that Suarez knew he owed the club. Rodgers said,

I'm sure he does know he owes Liverpool. You'll find that out once he gets that strip on – he'll work his socks off. He's received nothing but affection and love from the supporters. They deserve no less than a hundred per cent back and, knowing Luis, that's what he'll give them. I think he just can't wait to get playing again. There's a real determination in him now and obviously there was a lot going on over the course of the summer. But he's trained really hard, really well, and his entrance to come back into the squad now is perfect timing. We've got a few injuries and the big thing is he's now available. To have someone of that quality to come into the squad is good.

I do sense he is committed, absolutely. I think that's

the one thing about Luis because of the type of character he is, that when he plays football, he can't play it any other way. He knows what the club's stance was and he stayed. We stayed strong in our belief that we wanted to hang on to him. Of course it was difficult for everyone in the summer but that's behind us now. He's champing at the bit to get back.

Rodgers revealed that Suarez had sought and received excellent support and help after the Ivanovic bite incident, saying, 'He has had support in every way – not just technical and tactical development. We look at physical elements and how we can improve the psychological state. He has worked tirelessly on every aspect. He's had a long time to reflect on what has happened but now all that is in the past, the ban is finished and he has suffered because he hasn't been playing. Now he is available and we are all delighted he is ready to go again.'

Liverpool had lost just one match of the ten that Luis had missed – the final game of his ban, against Southampton. But it would be United, not Luis, who triumphed as he returned in the third-round tie of the League Cup (now known as the Capital Cup) at Old Trafford. A goal from United's own poacher, Javier 'Chicharito' Hernandez, killed off Luis's hopes of a victorious return as United went on to win 1–0. But Luis was cheered to the rafters by the mass of Liverpool fans in what used to be the 'Scoreboard End'. OK, he looked a little ring-rusty but he gradually imposed himself on the game and caused United's backline more than a few jitters with his darting runs and pace.

Rodgers was just delighted that his main man had returned and come through unscathed. He said, 'Luis was excellent. He did well considering how long he has been out. The adrenaline will have been pumping and it will take him one or two days to recover. He's a fighter and he will be ready for the weekend.'

The weekend match saw Luis and Liverpool travel north to Sunderland and they did not disappoint the army of fans who also made the journey. With Luis hitting form in his Premier League return, Liverpool ran out 3–1 winners. And Luis marked his return with two of those three goals – and later dedicated them to his newborn son, Benjamin. Luis was back – and in style – much to the delight of his Brazilian team-mate Lucas. 'Luis has just become a father again and, for him to celebrate with two goals, I am very happy for him,' Lucas told the *Liverpool Echo*. 'He is showing again just how good he is. He is a world-class player and it is so important to have players like that if you want to fight for good things this season. Hopefully he will have another fantastic season for us like he did last year.'

Lucas added that he also saw encouraging signs that the budding partnership between Luis and Daniel Sturridge could pay dividends for the club. 'When Dan arrived here, within a few months Luis got the ban so they didn't have much chance to play many games together. But you could see today how well they linked up. The understanding between them is really good and it will only get better. It will improve over the course of the season and hopefully they will keep helping us with goals and assists.'

Next up on the comeback trail for Luis was his return

in front of the Anfield faithful. He did not let them down, scoring his third goal in as many games and firing home the opening goal to help Liverpool beat Crystal Palace 3–1. Luis had set the tone for his big comeback by walking onto the pitch cradling baby son Benjamin in his arms and holding the hand of his three-year-old daughter, Delfina. He explained why he had walked on with his children to Uruguayan newspaper *El Pais*:

In England it is not common and at first the club told me I was not going to go on with them – but I told them that my children were going to come with me, like it or not. They understood in the end and it was a nice moment, a unique moment for me. My family make me think hard and calm me. Nowadays I think a lot of them when I'm on the field. I suffered a lot as a child and I do not want my children, or any other child, to experience the circumstances as I did. As a parent I try to give them all the love in the world and all the best.

He added, 'I am aware that in recent matches that I played I've been calmer. I am very self-critical and I realised that playing well, with more tranquility, is helping me a lot. I realise and I prefer to continue and not be the same as before.'

Luis also spoke about the dynamic role his captain Steven Gerrard had played in helping to keep him at the club. He said, 'Gerrard, for me, is a legend in Liverpool and a great team-mate that helped me a lot. His attitude was an extra boost for me to take the decision to stay in Liverpool; both he and the fans of Liverpool influenced much [of] that. I admire him for the great player he is worldwide. For me, he will always be a benchmark and at club level he is the best player I have played with in my career, as a person and as a footballer.'

The win put Liverpool a point clear of Arsenal at the top of the Premier League table as the club sent out an ominous warning about their ambitions for the season. Luis's strike partner Sturridge also got in on the act with a goal that meant he had hit nineteen goals in twenty-five games since joining from Chelsea the previous January. Similarly, Luis had scored nineteen in his last twenty-two games. This was a partnership that clearly had major potential and it would get better and better as the duo worked together as the season progressed. It was a partnership full of pace, invention – and plenty of goals. The pair would prove a nightmare to control for most Premier League defences as their understanding of each other improved.

After the win over Palace, Rodgers paid tribute to his two strikers and made it clear that there was much more to come from them because they were both 'on the same wavelength'. He said,

I've played them in a number of positions. I've played one of them up top and one of them in a semi-wide position, I've played Daniel through the middle and Luis in behind but Luis is not a number ten. They are both nine and a halves in terms of how they can get in between defenders, and can drop in short or go long.

They were exceptional today. In the first half in

particular, some of their combination play and their link-up was outstanding and they are right up there with the best in this league. They have that telepathic understanding. You are doing drills to improve that understanding, but I think top players are on the same wavelength and that's what they are.

Three weeks after his match-winning display against Palace, Luis proved he was really back in business by grabbing his fourth Premier League hat-trick – and his first in front of the Anfield faithful. Poor West Bromwich Albion were the hapless victims of his latest haul, suffering a 4–1 battering. Sturridge completed the goal rout, much to the delight of boss Rodgers, who was enjoying immensely the ever developing partnership of his two strikers. Rodgers said he believed Luis's run of goals was his way of thanking the club for standing by him, 'I knew once I got the commitment from him in the summer he wasn't going to walk out. He's been great from then on. It was a difficult summer for him but it was for everyone. But we managed it as a club and he managed himself well and he has come out of the other side and he is performing as he does, to a very high level.'

Even Rodgers' West Brom counterpart Steve Clarke was keen to praise Suarez and Sturridge. Clarke admitted, 'It was a difficult afternoon. We set ourselves up to be open but maybe we were a little bit too open. The first goal is disappointing to lose and the second goal is an unbelievable header from the edge of the box. We kept going – you can't fault the effort – but we gave ourselves too big a mountain to climb. At the moment their two boys up front are in form and we suffered for that.'

However, Luis would go on to surpass his hat-trick at the start of December as he notched FOUR goals against Norwich. That earned him a place in the record books as the first player ever to score three hat-tricks against the same club. It also meant he had hit eleven goals in five matches against the Canaries – little wonder that they dreaded playing against him and hoped against hope that his name would be absent from the team sheet whenever they lined up against the Reds.

Luis's first goal was, undoubtedly, the goal of the match as he unleashed an unstoppable strike from thirty-five yards out that left Norwich keeper John Ruddy with no chance. After the match, Brendan Rodgers was asked how Suarez's four-goal super-show rated. The Liverpool boss told Sky Sports,

Well, certainly I haven't seen better. It was a brilliant performance, just a pleasure to have watched that. Every goal was like a 'wow' goal, from the first right through to the end, so an incredible performance by an incredible player and, as I said, it was a real pleasure. I really enjoyed watching my team tonight. We were full of creativity and goals and worked very hard. You can't ask any more of Luis. He's certainly earned his money and [is] just a pleasure to work with. I think you see his happiness; he's really happy in his football and the whole club just is a hand-in-glove fit for him.

Liverpool skipper Steven Gerrard told the club's official website,

> You have seen a world-class performance, probably one of the best individual performances I've seen at Anfield – and I've been playing here a long time. Having worked with him every single day, it's probably less of a surprise to me as it is to the supporters. I've been pushing his corner for a long time that he is up there with the best in the world. I think he's getting so close to the main two, Ronaldo and Messi. If he keeps going, I think he can catch them. His fourth goal was average and it was a 30-yard free kick, so I think that sums his performance up.

Just eleven days after notching four against Norwich, Luis chalked up another milestone in his Liverpool career when he captained the club for the first time in a league game. It was a game that would long live in his memory – and not just because he was made skipper. Luis led Liverpool to a 5–0 win over Spurs – at Tottenham! Inevitably, he also got his name on the scoresheet, grabbing a brace as the Kop kings crushed their hosts. They were Luis's sixteenth and seventeenth goals of a season that was rapidly turning into the best ever of his glittering career. The win was also Liverpool's biggest ever at White Hart Lane, in a match that saw the hosts' Brazilian midfielder, Paulinho, sent off. Additionally, it would spell the end for Tottenham's manager, Andre Villas-Boas. The win was all the more remarkable as it was achieved without the services of Steven Gerrard and Daniel Sturridge.

Afterwards, Rodgers was all smiles as he said, 'We got five goals but it could have been eight. We were outstanding even though we were missing outstanding players. We've shown that the team is the most important thing to us.'

That was a view that Luis was keen to back. He said, 'I was a little surprised to be made captain but I think we have only one captain here – Steven Gerrard. If we stay together, we are together, we are the captain, the team is the captain, that's important. It's far more important than me being captain that we win 5–0 against Tottenham – this is very important.

'If we continue this level the next two or three weeks, we can win the league or we can finish in the top four. It's important we concentrate and focus on the next game.'

The day after the victory at Tottenham, Luis earned a further accolade when he was declared the winner of the Football Supporters' Federation Player of the Year award in London, beating off the likes of Manchester United's Robin van Persie for the honour. After collecting the award, Luis admitted that it had been the continued backing of the Liverpool fans that had been all-important to him in his work when he finally returned to action. He said,

After so many difficult moments I was able to win the supporters back and that was unbelievable when I came back to play. They helped me and that was important for me, for my confidence and for my family because they are together with me in this. This award is very special for me because my hard work on the pitch is recognised.

Everybody knows about my problems and my difficult year but after that I forgot everything and have been able to get back on the pitch. Liverpool are starting to reach their potential and we can play our best on the pitch. It's very important that we stay together.

Luis's wonderful December got better and better as it was revealed on the 20th of the month that he had signed a new contract at Liverpool. It was the surprise early Christmas present all Reds fans had been praying for: their best player was now tied up by the club for another four and a half years. His original deal was due to end in 2016 and the new contract meant he would earn £160,000 per week until the end of the 2013–14 season, rising to £200,000 per week over the remaining four years.

Luis said,

I am delighted to have agreed a new deal with Liverpool and have my future secured for the long term. We have some great players and the team is growing and improving all the time. I believe I can achieve the ambitions of winning trophies and playing at the very highest level with Liverpool. My aim is to help get us there as quickly as possible.

Without doubt the backing I have received from the Liverpool fans has influenced my decision. I am so proud to represent them and go out to do my best for them every time I pull on the shirt. We have a special relationship; they have love for me and in return I love them back. I will always do my best for them and hopefully we can achieve success together.

Brendan Rodgers also hailed the 'fantastic news' on the club's official website, saying, 'Luis is a world-class talent and securing his services is crucial for what we are trying to achieve here. What's most important and most exciting is that, at just 26 years old, his best years are still ahead of him and we now know we'll be seeing him reach that potential in a Liverpool shirt.'

Club owner John W. Henry was also delighted and said it showed how Liverpool FC was moving forwards: 'We are committed to working hard to keep our best players and this is an indication that we are moving in the right direction and moving at a pace that impresses one of the best players in world football. The club has made major strides forward in recent years and we are all committed to delivering the success our supporters want and deserve.'

On 1 January 2014 Luis was at it again – earning yet another page in the history books. His goal in the 2–0 home win over Hull got his New Year off to a rousing start, as it meant he had become the first Liverpool player to score twenty goals in successive Premier League seasons since Robbie Fowler in 1994–95 and 1995–96. The goal against Hull meant that Luis had scored fifteen goals in just seven Premier League appearances. I'm told that Luis was happy like the proverbial cat that got the cream after the match when made aware of his latest landmark and boss Rodgers was also purring with delight, although he was quick to point out that it had been a team effort. Rodgers said, 'It was arguably our best win of the season, on the back of what was a tough schedule for us with a light squad. The energy, as you'd expect, was not what it has been but we showed great resilience. Luis Suarez's quality is unquestionable. It's probably unfair that our team doesn't get the credit.

'Everyone talks about Luis and we all know he's a world-class player but, even when he was out of the team, we only lost one game. Today was a great team performance and what we're building here is based around that.'

Rodgers also revealed that Luis had gone through the pain barrier to spearhead Liverpool's bid for the three points against Hull, 'He had a real bad knock on the top of his foot from the Chelsea game. I know, having managed and worked with players, that most wouldn't have played with what he had today. He had strapping on it and he put himself out there for the team yet again. That's why he gets the goals that he does, because he's so determined.'

The fans on the Kop were certainly grateful to their magical number seven for playing and securing the points: they rated his goal as the best of the weekend and few would argue with that as Luis's free kick curled into the net from twenty yards out. That goal meant that he also became the joint-fastest player in Premier League history to reach twenty goals in a season, tying with Andy Cole. Cole, then at Newcastle, also scored his twentieth goal on a New Year's Day, back in 1994. But by hitting his twenty in just fifteen league matches, Luis also broke the record for fewest matches played to reach that number of goals.

By the first week of March 2014 Luis had fired Liverpool up into second place in the Premier League with his goals and his wonderful partnership with Daniel Sturridge. The duo had now earned the nickname of 'the SAS' – Suarez and Sturridge – as they caused all sorts of problems for hapless defenders with their pace, almost telepathic understanding and goals galore. By that stage of the season, Luis was the top scorer in the Premier League with twenty-four goals from twenty-three matches. He also led the way with assists, setting up ten goals.

The key to his exploits? He was settled and happy at Liverpool, as he explained to the gentlemen of the press before the team travelled thirty-five miles down the East Lancs Road for an encounter with their most bitter rivals, Manchester United, on Sunday, 16 March.

I'm twenty-seven, at my peak and feel very happy within the club because I'm part of the best football in the world: the Premier League. I'm enjoying every game I play and my family life here, which is very important. I like winning; I hate losing. I'm one of the best players in the world, so having the opportunity to win everything – and losing only occasionally – is what drives me. I'm ambitious. I want to win and won't stop until I score one, two or more goals. I want to enjoy the here and now. Every player should live in the present, to enjoy what they're doing. Thinking about things I did as a kid or at Ajax aren't going to improve me on the pitch. I want to stay in that position and look to the future. What happened in the past happened – you have to move on.

And moving on he had done – and was continuing to do. Luis was certainly looking forward to the United match at Old Trafford: it was another chance to show the watching world just how far he and Liverpool had come. The build-up was, inevitably, tense and the general feeling was that a Liverpool win at the home of the reigning champions would lay down a real marker; that, yes, they should now be seen as genuine title challengers and that the days of United's domination were, indeed, coming to an end.

Liverpool were definitely the form team of the two and you would have expected them to be firm favourites to win at Old Trafford. But the bookies were not so sure. Paddy Power believed United could spring a surprise.

Liverpool's title credentials are sure to face a stiff test when Brendan Rodgers' Reds make the trip to Old Trafford to take on David Moyes' Manchester United on Sunday afternoon. United – the defending champions – may have meekly surrendered their title this season but David Moyes' men have hinted at a return to some kind of form in recent weeks, having recorded back-to-back Premier League victories, albeit over relatively modest opposition.

The Red Devils would dearly love to puncture Liverpool's title challenge and the home side can be backed at 6/4 with Paddy Power to do just that by beating Brendan Rodgers' men this weekend. Those keen to side with the Red Devils should note a 'money back special' from Paddy Power, who will refund all first scorer, last scorer, correct score and scorecast bets should United striker Wayne Rooney find the net against the Reds this weekend.

But it would be Liverpool who came out on top in a one-sided affair, winning 3–0 to cement their position in the top four – and those all-important Champions League spots – and killing off United's faint hopes of doing the same. Two penalties from Steven Gerrard and, inevitably, a goal from Luis left United and their fans in bits. And that's without even mentioning the third penalty that the skipper missed, plus Nemanja Vidic's sending-off as he and United were run ragged by the brilliant visitors.

It could have been 7–0 and United wouldn't have had much room for complaint. It was the day when Liverpool proved once and for all that they were back in business at the very top of English football as they nonchalantly brushed aside the challenge of the fallen champions. This was why Luis had signed for Liverpool and it was all he had ever wanted when he signed: to play for a top club, a club that could compete for the Premier League and the Champions League crowns.

Luis Suarez had become the all-round complete striker. He scored goals, he ran centre-halves dizzy and he now rarely moaned or got involved in controversy. Even his previous reputation as a diver was history. As the *Daily Mail*'s brilliant football writer Martin Samuel summed up, 'It was just three minutes old when Daniel Sturridge had his first crack at goal and only five minutes had gone when the visitors should have had their first penalty. It is a familiar scene now, the referee waving away an appeal from Suarez only for the replay to show the Uruguayan was more than justified. Yes, he used to dive, but he doesn't any more. Can't they accept that now, and start treating him like the other strikers?'

Luis had grown up as a man and a player. As Brendan Rodgers said before the match,

Over the years, people get called 'hard men'. They're normally centre-halves or midfield players. But Suarez is a hard man. Don't underestimate him; he's a hard man, even though he's a striker. He gets battered every game, he gets kicked. He's probably the toughest player mentally I've ever come across in my life. He's the most relentless in his desires. We've seen it in all his time here. He's maturing as well. There's not much rattles him and plenty that inspires him.

The greatest thing is that it's about his football now. It was a real difficult period for him in the summer. It took a lot of work to convince him that the club's going forward.

We won a big battle in keeping him here. But he's at his happiest now. He became a father for the second time, he's twenty-seven, he's got a World Cup to look forward to. I just think this is a club that suits him.

Luis was buzzing after the game. He knew how big the win was to Liverpool FC and their loyal fans; how they'd had to suffer over the years as United notched up league title after league title. Now the order at the top of the English game was finally changing, with Liverpool back at the summit. The win meant they were second in the table, just four points behind leaders Chelsea but with a game in hand.

After the win Luis threw himself on the Old Trafford turf and walked off arm in arm with his skipper, punching the air in delight and beaming with joy. Gerrard summed up the mood in the Liverpool dressing room and on the coach on the way back down the East Lancs Road: 'I have come here many times before and been played off the park,' he said. '[Manchester United] are a fantastic team and this is one of the most difficult places to come in the Premier League. We've come here and dominated from start to finish, yet we're still going away slightly disappointed that we didn't score more goals. We will enjoy this but we'll need to move on quickly. The easiest thing in football is to talk the talk. We have to treat Cardiff and Sunderland the same as Manchester United. We believe that we can win the league.'

Those last eight words were what Liverpool fans had dreamed of hearing for two decades – now their challenge was real and powerful. As Luis and his team-mates approached the final straight in their 2013–14 Premier League campaign, the dream seemed on: a first top-flight title since 1990. But before we analyse how Luis fared in the latter stages of the 2013–14 campaign, let's take a closer look at how his exploits as a marauding striker who was doing the business up front with Daniel Sturridge gave credence to the growing belief that the duo were heading towards a legendary status at Anfield – a status some of their illustrious predecessors had achieved.

CHAPTER FOURTEEN

IN THE FOOTSTEPS
OF LEGENDS

During his time at Anfield, Luis Suarez was asked to form a partnership with two of the top English strikers of the modern era: two strikers with very different capabilities and ways of playing the game. First up was Andy Carroll, the big man brought in by Dalglish in the same 2011 transfer window that saw Luis arrive at the club. Carroll and Suarez were a Little & Large combo that Kenny hoped would see Luis feeding off the knockdowns provided by the big man. Of course, Carroll also wasn't bad playing it on the ground either.

Then, when Kenny departed, Brendan Rodgers came in and had a clear vision of Luis playing up front with a different partner in a more flexible arrangement. Rodgers dispensed with the services of big man Carroll and brought in the lightning-fast, tricky, silky skills of Daniel Sturridge. A different set-up but the aim was the same as Dalglish's – to find a partner with whom Luis could click, a partnership that would take the club to new heights of glory.

Just, in fact, as some great forward duos had done in the distant and not too distant past at Liverpool. Dalglish had underlined his own assessment of how Suarez would fit into the new dream team he was building by giving him the legendary number-seven shirt – the shirt made famous by the likes of himself and Kevin Keegan. Former Kop hero Phil Thompson believed that Suarez was a modern-day model from the Keegan/Dalglish prototype. He said of Suarez, 'He excites me and he's a player between Kenny Dalglish and Kevin Keegan, that bundle of enthusiasm. Hopefully he can do it for Liverpool.'

Suarez, Sturridge and Carroll were certainly walking in the footsteps of legends as they tried to become Anfield heroes. There had been no shortage of wonderful Liverpool FC double acts and striking giants if the modern-day trio wanted to examine the history books for inspiration.

Carroll, for example, was not the first Geordie to arrive at Anfield for a British record transfer fee. No, that accolade goes to Albert Stubbins, who signed from Newcastle for the then record fee of £12,500 in 1946.

Like Andy, he was born on Tyneside and was similarly worshipped by the Newcastle fans after racking up a series of scoring feats. He first appeared for the Toon in 1937, scoring 6 goals in 30 games but he also grabbed another 188 in just 231 matches for Newcastle during the Second World War.

To the Gallowgate faithful he was a hero and they were just as stunned as their modern counterparts were over the sale of Andy Carroll when their club agreed to sell Big Albert to Liverpool. But it would be at Liverpool that he would chalk up his greatest and most enduring successes. Indeed, the outcome of his first season on Merseyside would guarantee he would always be viewed affectionately at Liverpool FC, for he helped the club to their first league title in twenty-four years (since the 1922–23 season). It was the fifth time in their history that the club had been league champions and Stubbins was feted for his twenty-four goals, which had helped bring the title home.

It was now that he established the partnership that would become the prototype for the Keegan/Toshack, Dalglish/Rush and Carroll/Suarez models. Stubbins, the big, bullish traditional centre-forward, found an ally in Jackie Balmer, who had started out as a centre-forward but found a better home for his more subtle skills as an inside-forward. He became more of a number ten (or number seven, if we are thinking of Dalglish and Keegan) and his silkier skills were the perfect foil for the bruising Stubbins.

Like Dalglish, Keegan and, more recently, Suarez, he was also no slouch in front of goal. Indeed, in that debut season partnership with Stubbins, Balmer matched the centre-forward by grabbing twenty-four goals himself. Together, the two of them had contributed forty-eight goals to that first league-title crown in twenty-four years.

Unlike Stubbins, Balmer was a local lad – born in West Derby, Liverpool – and played for Everton as an amateur before signing pro forms for then Liverpool manager George Patterson in 1935. Balmer also created his own little piece of footballing history at the time by scoring a hat-trick of hat-tricks in that triumphant 1946–47 season. He grabbed the first on 9 November 1946, in the 3–0 home win over Portsmouth, with the goals coming in the thirtieth (a penalty), seventieth and eighty-first minutes.

A week later he even went one better, scoring all four in the 4–1 win over Derby County at the Baseball Ground. The feat included the hat-trick in six minutes – with goals on forty-three, forty-seven and forty-nine minutes – and the icing on the cake: the fourth goal on the hour.

Balmer would go down in history on 23 November 1946, when he hit the third of the three hat-tricks in the 4–2 home win over Arsenal. The goals came in the fifteenth, sixty-first and sixty-eighth minutes, with his partner-in-crime Stubbins scoring the fourth on seventy-eight minutes. That Stubbins' goal ended Balmer's remarkable run of ten consecutive goals but the inside-forward wasn't finished yet: he claimed five more goals in his next four games, for a total of fifteen in seven matches.

Balmer had equalled the record of Everton's Dixie Dean, who had scored three hat-tricks in a row. But Dean's feat had not been achieved in one single campaign. The Toffees' centre-forward had scored two in the final two games of the 1927–28 season and one at the start of the following campaign.

In the 2007–08 season Fernando Torres would score consecutive hat-tricks at Anfield (against Middleborough on 23 February 2008 and West Ham on 5 March 2008), becoming the first person to achieve that feat since Balmer. Torres's comments afterwards show just how highly Balmer's record sixty years earlier is still rated at Anfield. Torres had said, 'I only learned of the record after the game and it is a big honour for me. This club has a wonderful history so to be a part of that is very special and it is something I am very proud of. But it is also a record for everyone at the club because it would be impossible for me to score goals if it was not for my team-mates, the manager, the coaching staff, everyone.'

Even then boss Rafa Benitez hailed the legendary achievement of Balmer all those years previously while also praising his Spanish striker for his modern-day feat. Benitez said, 'This club is built on legend. For Fernando to score hat-tricks in consecutive home games is a fantastic achievement and everyone at the club is very proud of that.'

Balmer was made skipper in the 1947–48 season and continued to score for fun along with Stubbins. Altogether he played a total of 309 games, scoring 110 goals between 1935 and 1952 before retiring that year. He died on Christmas Day, 1984, aged sixty-eight.

Liverpool fans mourned his passing but he had never been as big an idol at Anfield as Stubbins. He refused to throw himself into tackles and that alienated him with some fans. Balmer would say, 'They were entitled to their opinion. Maybe I didn't go in for the crunch tackle but that kind of thing wasn't my idea of football. I was never a coward at the game but I got a shudder when I saw the boot going in.'

Stubbins was a much more wholehearted character, who loved to fight for his beloved Liverpool. In his second season at the club, he nicked twenty-four league goals, including four when Huddersfield came to Anfield on 6 March 1948. An illustration of his mental and physical toughness was that he played and scored those four goals despite receiving a threatening telegram on the morning of the match.

Stubbins revealed, 'On the morning of the match I received a telegram and, although I can't remember the exact wording, the general consensus was if I scored, my legs would be broken. I didn't want to worry the rest of the team so I kept it to myself. It was obviously meant to frighten me but it didn't work. I never did find out who sent it. Perhaps it was George Kay's [the then manager] way of geeing me up!'

Stubbins would make a total of 178 appearances for Liverpool, scoring 83 goals. He helped the club to reach the 1950 FA Cup Final against Arsenal, when at Wembley he led the attack, though not fully recovered from an injury. It would prove a day of disappointment, as Liverpool went down 2–0, with both goals scored by Ray Lewis. An interesting side note to that final was that the great Bob Paisley was famously dropped for the game – even after scoring one of the goals in the 2–0 semi-final win over Everton. That decision, Paisley would later admit, almost led to his leaving the club.

The last of Stubbins's first-team appearances was at Stoke on 3 January 1953. He died on 28 December 2002, aged eighty-two. The Geordie boy who had come to Liverpool, treading the path that Andy Carroll would also follow, died a legend at his adopted club. The extent of his impact on Merseyside – and the love for him – is also seen in the fact that his image made the sleeve of the Beatles' most famous album. As the *Guardian* put it in a fine obituary,

On the sleeve of the Beatles' *Sergeant Pepper's Lonely Hearts Club Band* is the image of a footballer: Albert Stubbins in his Liverpool heyday, red shirt, red hair. He was a hero to thousands of Liverpool fans and, intriguingly, to fans of his original club, Newcastle United. Indeed, it might be said that Stubbins's fame has actually increased on Tyneside since his retirement, long ago...

Liverpool were unquestionably lucky to get him. He had asked Newcastle for a transfer, and at least 18 clubs had made inquiries. Liverpool, using a recognised centre-half, Bill Jones, at centre-forward, had just been thrashed by Manchester United in an early 1946–47 league game when they beat all opposition to Stubbins's transfer.

The *Independent*'s obituary was similarly eloquent in summing up the man who had become the first post-war hero of the Kop. Written by Ivan Ponting, it read,

The flame-haired north-easterner, loved on both Tyneside and Merseyside for his unfailingly equable approach to the game almost as much as for his prolific exploits with Newcastle United and Liverpool, was chosen by the Beatles as one of sixty-three famous faces to adorn the artwork of their ground-breaking *Sgt. Pepper's Lonely Hearts Club Band* in 1967. Wearing a characteristic broad grin, he is wedged cosily among the likes of Marlene Dietrich, Lewis Carroll and Karl Marx, and it is a tribute to his stature in popular culture that he doesn't seem the slightest bit out of place.

A ball-playing centre-forward, endowed with subtle skills, searing pace and a scorching shot in both of his size-11 boots – though he was quite tall, the immensity of his feet was rather incongruous in such a slender fellow – Stubbins was not merely a taker, but also a maker of goals. He led his forward line intelligently, constantly seeking to bring colleagues into play with his perceptive passing and for all his dead-eyed menace it was clear that he enjoyed his work, his nickname of 'The Smiling Assassin' being singularly apt.

It was also apt that in 1967, on the release of *Sgt. Pepper*, Liverpudlian legend Paul McCartney sent Stubbins a copy of the album with a personal message: 'Well done, Albert, for all those glorious years of football. Long may you bob and weave.'

Stubbins would also link up with another hero of the terraces at Liverpool: the great Billy Liddell, the man who would earn his club the moniker 'Liddellpool' because of his regular brilliant exploits on their behalf. Liddell could also play as a foil to the big striker but in that championship-winning season of 1946 –47 he was darting down the left wing, scoring seven goals himself in thirty-four games and also setting up Stubbins and Balmer with many outstanding crosses. Billy also played a key role in getting Stubbins to Wembley in that 1950 FA Cup final, scoring the second goal (after Paisley's opener) in the semi against Everton. Like Paisley, Liddell was Scottish and the two would share a lifetime's friendship.

In his 1990 book, *My 50 Golden Reds*, Paisley would sum up Liddell like this:

Bill was always strong, even as a teenager, and was a naturally two-footed player. He also had good skills, but was so strong for a winger. In those days most wingers were fairly lightly built players but Bill had absolutely no fear. He was a gentleman through and through. But he would also work on the pitch. He was a real workhorse but he had a nice touch as well. Sometimes he would use his strength to send defenders flying, but always totally fairly.

It is close between him and Kenny [Dalglish] for the title of the best player ever to have worn a Liverpool shirt. By today's standards, I don't think there is the money to buy a Billy Liddell.

Liddell was a one-club man. He signed for Liverpool, aged sixteen, in 1938 and retired in 1961, having scored 228 goals in 534 matches, and was the club's leading goal-scorer in 8 out of 9 seasons from 1949 to 1958. By 1957 he had surpassed the club appearance record set by the great Elisha Scott. He became the club's oldest ever goal-scorer and, after King Kenny, is the second oldest player to have represented Liverpool. He died in 2001, aged seventy-nine.

Billy Liddell had become a legend for his exploits and he had been loved and respected by his colleagues at the club. Years earlier, Bill Shankly had summed up Billy's physical strength, saying, 'Liddell was some player... He had everything. He was fast, powerful, shot with either foot and his headers were like blasts from a gun. On top of all that he was as hard as granite. What a player! He was so strong – and he took a nineteen-inch collar shirt!'

And his old team-mate Stubbins was also in awe of his talent:

We were playing Preston at Deepdale and got a free kick just outside the box. Billy was aiming to hit it with his right foot when the wind rolled the ball away. He just let it run and hit it with his left and it went in like a rocket. He was fast, courageous and very strong. When we got to Newcastle one day, I popped into their dressing room to say hello to my old team-mates. Newcastle had a very good full-back in Bobby Cowell, who said to me, 'Albert, how do I play against Billy Liddell?' I replied, 'I'll say one thing, if Billy picks up the ball and you're not close to him when he does, you're dead!'

Liverpool legend Roy Evans was just grateful that he had met his hero: 'He was a great figurehead for Liverpool Football Club in an era when you didn't really have stars as such, but he was a very moderate and humble man. I was lucky enough to meet and get to know Billy quite well in later years. He was the exception to the rule that says you should never meet your heroes and was a truly great man.'

And Billy's old mate Bob Paisley was another who was knocked out by his physical prowess: 'Bill was so strong it was unbelievable. You couldn't shake him off the ball. It didn't matter where he was playing, though I suppose his best position was outside-left. He could go round you, or past you, or even straight through you sometimes!'

Even his English rival Sir Alf Ramsey, boss of England's World Cup winners in 1966, had only good words for this remarkable man. Talking about how he dreaded facing him in his playing days, Ramsey admitted, 'I always knew I was in for a hectic afternoon when I was marking Billy. The only way to try to hold him was to beat him to possession of the ball. Once he had it, he was difficult to stop.'

Three years after Liddell's death a permanent memorial to him was unveiled at Anfield by his widow Phyllis and fellow Anfield legend Ian Callaghan. The plaque pays tribute to a man who dedicated his life to Liverpool FC. In 2006 he was acclaimed by Liverpool fans, who voted him sixth in a poll entitled '100 Players Who Shook The Kop'. The poll was massive and emphatic – attracting 110,000 supporters, who all nominated their favourite Top 10 players.

Further acclaim befell Billy in November 2008 when he was finally inducted into the Scottish Football Hall of Fame.

After Billy retired, two new goal kings emerged in the Anfield pantheon of fame, who would resurrect the Little & Large combo established by Stubbins and Balmer: the twin striking partnership that would become a mainstay of Liverpool's play throughout the years, leading to the eventual link-up of Carroll and Suarez.

This time the number-nine shirt would be worn by the little man, while the bigger, more traditional target man would take the number-eight shirt. Yes, step forward Ian St John and

Roger Hunt – an Anglo-Scots partnership made in heaven that would propel Liverpool forward during the 1960s. St John was a proud Scotsman and was just 5ft 8in in his football boots yet he had a terrific leap on him, a clever footballing brain, was very brace and he knew where the net was. He would also turn provider for Hunt as the years went by, selflessly scoring fewer goals himself.

Ian St John was born in Motherwell, Lanarkshire in 1938 and arrived at Liverpool FC in 1961 from his hometown football club. Bill Shankly splashed out £37,500 to bring the wee man south – a fee that was more than double Liverpool's previous transfer record. The twenty-three-year-old settled in quickly – so quickly that he became an idol of the Kop in his very first game!

In that debut, St John hit a hat-trick against Liverpool's city rivals Everton. It was not enough to save his new team from going down 4–3 in the Liverpool Senior Cup Final but it was enough to have the fans chanting his name. Any player who scored a hat-trick against their bitter local rivals would have earned that accolade.

'Saint', as he would become known, made his official debut in the 2–0 victory at Bristol Rovers in August 1961. At the time Liverpool were floundering in the Second Division, although that was all about to change under the auspices of Shankly, backed up by inspirational signings like St John and the grooming of local youngsters into the first team. They had been stuck in the Second Division for six long years but now, with Saint in the team, that was about to end. In his very first season at the club, they were promoted to the top flight, finishing the campaign as champions, eight points clear of second-placed Leyton Orient.

Saint scored his first goals at the end of August 1961, grabbing a brace in the thirty-ninth and ninetieth minutes of a 4–1 win over Sunderland at Roker Park. But just as significantly, his new strike partner, Roger Hunt, pulled off the same feat as Liverpool roared home. It was to be the start of a wonderful partnership that would take Liverpool to the very top. That debut season brought a goals return of eighteen from Saint in forty league matches.

His second campaign at the club was just as eventful – they finished eighth in the league but made the FA Cup semi-finals, where only a defiant show by the brilliant Gordon Banks saw them lose to Leicester City. Saint's contribution saw him finish the campaign with a total of twenty-two goals in all competitions.

But it would be in his third season at Anfield that he really proved his worth, as the club finally won the First Division title again, for the sixth time but the first in twenty-seven long years. Ian chipped in with twenty-one league goals, the highest number he would ever chalk up in his time at the club. The club had won the title with four points to spare over second-placed Manchester United, with deposed champions Everton third.

The glory years continued for Saint as the following season he helped Liverpool to fill the one gaping hole in the club's list of domestic honours: the FA Cup. Not only did Saint help them lift the FA Cup, he won it for them. The final was an epic encounter between Shankly's Liverpool and Don Revie's Leeds

United. With the score at 0–0 after ninety minutes, it became the first final since 1947 to go to extra time.

Leeds' well-drilled defence had kept Liverpool at bay for ninety-three minutes but they started to tire. It was then that Saint's partner-in-crime Roger Hunt struck, finally breaking the deadlock with a stooping header from a cross by left-back Gerry Byrne, who had played most of the match with a broken collar bone.

Liverpool now laid siege to the Tykes' goal but, somehow, Leeds repelled their attacks and managed to get back in the game as Billy Bremner equalised with a half-volley. However, Liverpool continued to pile on the pressure and, in the 113th minute, Saint broke Leeds' hearts and sent Liverpool fans into ecstasy as he headed home from an Ian Callaghan cross. Leeds had no reply – Liverpool had won the FA Cup for the first time in their history, thanks to Ian St John.

More glory surfaced in the following campaign (1965–66) as Ian contributed ten goals in forty-one games to help the club win back their League title, finishing six points clear of Leeds. But disappointment followed the end of the league campaign when Saint returned to his native Scotland to play for Liverpool in the European Cup Winners' Cup final at Glasgow's Hampden Park. He and Liverpool crashed 2–1 in their first ever European final to German outfit Borussia Dortmund. Roger Hunt had cancelled out Siegfried Held's opener but a goal by Reinhard Libuda in the 109th minute won the trophy for the Germans. Liverpool lined up that day this way: 1 Tommy Lawrence, 2 Chris Lawler, 3 Gerry Byrne, 4 Gordon Milne, 5 Ron Yeats (captain), 6 Willie Stevenson, 7

Ian Callaghan, 8 Roger Hunt, 9 Ian St John, 10 Tommy Smith, 11 Peter Thompson.

Saint finished his Liverpool career in August 1971. He had played 425 games and scored 118 goals for the club. He played for Coventry for one season after leaving and then a season for Tranmere, before retiring as a player in 1973. But he was not finished with the game; he went on to manage at Motherwell (1973–74) and Portsmouth (1974–77) and in 1979 he forged a successful TV punditry career with Jimmy Greaves. The duo became known as Saint and Greavsie and had their own show until 1992.

Roger Hunt, his strike partner at Anfield during the glory years, would play the Sturridge/Carroll role to Saint's Suarez. He had joined the club three years earlier than Saint, in 1958, although he was just a month younger. Hunt thrived when St John arrived. With Ian in tandem setting him up and playing the perfect foil, Roger scored forty-one goals in forty-one league matches, including five hat-tricks, in their debut season together – the promotion-winning season of 1961–62. Those five hat-tricks came against Leeds United, Walsall, Swansea and his former clubs Bury and Middlesbrough.

The goals continued to flow in 1963–64 and 1965–66 as Liverpool became First Division champions. Hunt was the club's top scorer for eight consecutive seasons from 1962 to 1969 – and the goals came at crucial moments in the club's history. He would net four times in the 1964–65 FA Cup run, which saw West Bromwich Albion, Stockport County, Bolton Wanderers, Leicester City and Chelsea all defeated as Liverpool reached the final for the first time since 1950. As we have mentioned, in that final against Leeds, after a goal-less ninety minutes, Hunt scored the opener on ninety-three minutes, with strike pal Saint grabbing the winner – and he netted Liverpool's consolation in the 1966 European Cup Winners' Cup defeat to Borussia Dortmund.

Of course, 1966 was memorable for another reason for the man the Kop dubbed 'Sir Roger'. Yes, he won the World Cup with England at Wembley Stadium in that 4–2 triumph over West Germany. He had played in all six of England's games in the competition and scored three goals.

Hunt left the club to join Bolton Wanderers in December 1969 having made a wonderful contribution. He had played in 492 games and scored 286 goals. Only Ian Rush has since surpassed his goal-scoring total for Liverpool, though Rushie scored fewer League goals than Hunt, who still holds that record at the club.

Hunt was inducted into the English Football Hall of Fame in 2006 and was voted in at number thirteen by Liverpool fans on the 100 Players Who Shook The Kop poll. But perhaps the finest tribute to Hunt came from former Kop idol John Aldridge who, in September 2010, told the *Liverpool Daily Post* that he had chosen to wear the number- eight shirt at the club because of his admiration for Roger. Aldo said,

Being a striker it was only natural and inevitable that a Liverpool player in the same position would become my favourite. It was Roger Hunt. I simply loved him. His record was unbelievable too, 286 goals in 492 appearances is brilliant. Sadly it is rarely talked about now. He did amazing things for Liverpool and was one of the club's best ever players.

People suggested I didn't want to wear nine at Liverpool because it had been Ian Rush's number and I wouldn't be able to handle the pressure that came with it. That was rubbish. I wore number eight whenever I could. I always wanted to be number eight because of Roger Hunt. He was my idol.

And so to the 1970s and the partnership many pundits felt could have been the closest to that Carroll/Suarez link-up. Yes, the Kevin Keegan/John Toshack combo. Liverpool great Jamie Carragher predicted Andy and Luis COULD be a modern version when they linked up. The former defender told talkSPORT, 'The club made a big statement by bringing them in. Suarez made a great start with the first goal, so that's out the way now. But it was his performance more than anything that I think bodes well for the future. Also with Carroll coming back it looks, in essence, a perfect partnership.

'It was great for Liverpool in the past but obviously we're looking to the future now. If they have as big an impact on the club [as Keegan and Toshack], we'll have done very well.'

Big John Toshack started his career at Cardiff City, spending four years there from the age of sixteen, before moving to Liverpool in 1970. 'Tosh' was already a full Welsh international but some fans on the Kop still grumbled when Bill Shankly paid £110,000 for his services. They felt the fee was too high for a Welsh lad who was unproven at the very top level.

But Shanks had seen enough in him – and in his partnership with the smaller Brian Clark – to convince him that the lad could deliver the goods if he was nurtured and the right, smaller strike partner (in the mould of Clark) was found for him.

It didn't take long for the doubters to see it Shanks's way. Tosh made his debut on 14 November 1970, three days after signing, in the 0–0 draw with Coventry at Anfield but he really made his mark just a week after that in the Merseyside derby at Anfield. It was 0–0 at half-time but Everton had taken a 2–0 lead minutes into the second half.

Then came an amazing fightback in which Tosh would certainly play his part. Steve Heighway pulled a goal back on sixty-nine minutes and Tosh equalised seven minutes later, much to his delight as he celebrated his goal in front of the Kop. It wasn't over – Chris Lawler hit the winner six minutes from time and the crowd – and Big John – went wild. In just his second match, he had scored, helped Liverpool to a massive win over their neighbours and secured bragging rights for his new fans until at least the next derby clash.

He had made a claim for a place in the heart of the Liverpool fans but would have to wait until Keegan arrived the following season to truly cement it.

After scoring in that Mersey derby, Tosh claimed another league goal in the 1–1 home draw with Leeds in early December 1970.

Then he proved he meant business – that he believed he should now secure a permanent place in the first team – by scoring three goals in successive games. He hit the back of the net in the 2–0 triumph over Arsenal in late January and in the 1–0 wins over Leeds and West Ham in early February.

OK, five goals in twenty-one League games meant he hadn't set the world on fire in that debut season but it was not a bad return considering Shankly had not yet brought in the small man he believed could bring out the very best in Big John.

Tosh and Liverpool finished fifth in the league and the fans enjoyed a day trip down to London for the FA Cup final against Arsenal at Wembley. Tosh started the match but could not prevent the Kop kings losing 2–1 to Charlie George's killer winner in the 111th minute. Indeed, all three goals came in extra time. Steve Heighway had opened the scoring for Liverpool with a low drive that eluded keeper Bob Wilson. Eddie Kelly equalised and George wrecked Liverpool's dream with the goal that took the double (the league title and FA Cup) to Highbury – the first double achieved by any club since Tottenham Hotspur's double in 1961.

Tosh lined up that day in a Liverpool team that read: 1 Ray Clemence, 2 Chris Lawler, 3 Alec Lindsay, 4 Tommy Smith (captain), 5 Larry Lloyd, 6 Emlyn Hughes, 7 Ian Callaghan, 8 Alun Evans, 9 Steve Heighway, 10 John Toshack, 11 Brian Hall.

Heighway may have worn number nine but he played his magic essentially down the left wing, so number eight, Alun Evans, was essentially the foil to Tosh that day. But Shanks knew that he needed someone better equipped to play the little-man role to Tosh's giant if Liverpool were to progress even further.

Yet initially, that man didn't seem to be Kevin Keegan. No, Shanks liked what he saw when he watched Keegan at Scunthorpe United but the little man was playing as a creative midfielder in the lower leagues. The Liverpool manager initially had a similar role in mind for him at Anfield, with the hope that he might one day replace the long-serving Ian Callaghan in that role. But Shanks would change his mind when he saw Keegan in action in pre-season training. Then he realised that Kevin, with his tricky skills and natural eye for goal, was actually the answer to a bigger problem he needed to solve –the problem of who could be the perfect foil for Toshack.

Keegan signed in August 1971 from Scunthorpe. He was twenty years old and had cost £35,000 – it would seem like small change when he struck up what seemed an almost telepathic partnership with Toshack, and Shanks would later describe it as 'robbery with violence'.

Tosh, the big man, would win the ball in the air and plant it on the ground for the man who would become known by many as 'Mighty Mouse' to regularly lash home on the ground. Keegan would be the making of Toshack at Liverpool but Liverpool FC would certainly be the making of Kevin Keegan. In his six-year spell at Anfield he won a clutch of top medals, including three First Division titles, two UEFA Cups, one FA Cup and the European Cup. The move to Liverpool also gave him the confidence to become a regular in the England national team and set him up for more glory on a continental scale when he moved to German outfit Hamburg in 1977 (he would be crowned European Footballer of the Year in 1978 and 1979).

But it was for his link-up with Tosh that he will always be best remembered. Together the duo were unstoppable and even earned another sobriquet from the football magazine *Shoot*, who dubbed them Batman and Robin and took pictures of them in Dynamic Duo-style costumes.

Keegan made his Liverpool debut on 14 August 1971, partnering Toshack up front after their impressive pre-season work together. Kevin scored after twelve minutes in the 3–1 First Division win over Nottingham Forest at Anfield. The team that day read: Ray Clemence, Chris Lawler, Alec Lindsay, Tommy Smith, Larry Lloyd, Emlyn Hughes, Kevin Keegan, Peter Thompson, Steve Heighway, John Toshack, John McLaughlin.

Shanks knew Keegan was a special talent and that he was the man he had been looking for up front. He now abandoned any plans to play him in midfield.

It was a typical genius decision by a genius manager. Just how good a decision became clear two years after Keegan had signed. During those years his partnership with Tosh continued to blossom and in 1973 the pair helped Liverpool to the Division One title and the UEFA Cup. In the latter, Liverpool won the first leg against Borussia Mönchengladbach 3–0 but went down 2–0 in the return in Germany. It meant the first leg triumph – with two goals from Keegan – was enough. Liverpool had won 3–2 on aggregate and Keegan, who was the hero of the hour, had even missed a penalty!

The following year the Keegan/Toshack combination brought the FA Cup to Anfield for the first time as Liverpool beat Newcastle 3–0. As in the UEFA Cup final of the previous season, Keegan grabbed a match-winning brace. Of course, the match would also eventually be remembered for another reason: it was the last game in charge of Liverpool for the man who had gambled on Keegan and Toshack – the great Bill Shankly, who would be succeeded by coach Bob Paisley.

In 1977, his last season with Liverpool, Keegan helped the club to their finest hour: their first European Cup triumph. His mate Tosh was missing from the final line-up that wondrous night in Rome on 25 May. Tosh had become injured earlier in the campaign and had to sit out the latter part of the season.

Of course, he was there in Rome cheering on his partner-in-crime against Borussia Mönchengladbach – and Kevin did not let him or the millions of Liverpool fans watching worldwide down. Eight minutes from time, with the score at 2–1 to Liverpool and nerves starting to jangle, Keegan darted into the German box, only to be fouled by Berti Vogts. Fullback Phil Neal made no mistake with the ensuing penalty and Liverpool ran out 3–1 winners.

Keegan now departed for Germany, to join Hamburg while Toshack stayed at Anfield to try to get back to full fitness. But he only managed four games the next season and decided to leave for his first job in management, as player-manager at Swansea. It was as if Keegan's exit had effectively spelled the end for Toshack too.

Toshack had played 247 games in his 7½ years at Anfield, scoring 96 goals. Keegan had played in 323 games and hit 100 goals.

Later the two men admitted they loved their time together

as a partnership and paid tribute to each other's role in it. Toshack said, 'Myself and Kevin Keegan worked up a good understanding and as a partnership we flourished. We seemed to hit it off from almost day one and then got better and better as time went by.'

And Keegan said, 'Tosh was a wonderful player to play alongside. His aerial ability was fantastic and I always knew that he was going to win the high balls. From then on it was just a question of me reading which way the ball was going to go and from those situations we created many chances. I always admired Tosh's honesty as a player. He was a nice approachable lad and he did a really great job for the club during his time here.'

The fans of today still remember them as a 'dream team' ticket and, when Carroll and Suarez signed, were confident the pair would replicate that partnership. One Liverpool fan on a message board summed it up in this way:

This is a classic Toshack/Keegan partnership and, despite a few people talking about us playing the long ball game, this would never happen under Dalglish.

Those of us who remember know that although wingers are essential to the Toshack/Keegan formation, it cannot be the only option or we become predictable and easy to defend against. The key is to maintain pass and move football giving options down the wings or through the middle. In the long run we do need better quality wingers but for now we will have enough to provide attacking options for all scenarios. Suarez, Gerrard, Meireles will all offer Dalglish-type football through the middle while Johnson, Cole, Aurelio and Kelly can provide the width for now.

And another fan added, 'Carroll will obviously have to go some to emulate Toshack, but he has the same physical stature to intimidate defenders. Suarez is a very good footballer and a winner – this is what we need.

'So what if we shelled out a bit extra – we needed to and, by all accounts, we can afford it. Let the detractors drink their bitter with huge swigs!'

Toshack was voted in at number thirty-four on the 100 Players Who Shook The Kop poll while Keegan was eighth. Which brings us even closer to the modern day with arguably Liverpool's greatest ever strike combination – the brilliant Kenny Dalglish allied with the prolific goal-scoring talent of Ian Rush. If Toshack and Keegan were the prototype for the Suarez/Carroll axis, Rush and Dalglish would surely be the base for the Suarez/Sturridge combo. And Suarez and Sturridge proved they were worth every penny of their combined £37 million transfer fees as they evoked memories of the Rush/Dalglish axis with some tremendous goals during the 2013-14 campaign.

To this day, Rush remains the club's record goal-scorer, scoring 346 goals during his Liverpool career in 660 games. He also holds the record for the most goals in a season, hitting forty-seven in all competitions during the 1983–84 season. In the 100 Players who Shook the Kop poll, Rush finished third, behind only Steven Gerrard (second) and, inevitably, Kenny Dalglish in top position. Rush signed for Liverpool when he was eighteen in April 1980, though he had to remain at his first club, Chester, until the end of the season, as the transfer deadline had passed. Kop boss Bob Paisley splashed out £300,000 for his services – then a record fee for a teenager.

Ironically, his Liverpool debut came on 13 December, standing in for an injured Kenny Dalglish (his future strike-partner and, at the time, one of the most highly rated strikers in the world), and wearing his famous number-seven shirt in a First Division fixture at Portman Road against Ipswich Town.

It was hardly a case of trumpeting the arrival of a potential goal genius. Indeed, *The Times* perfectly summed up the general disinterest in Rush's debut, with a piece that highlighted that the loss of Dalglish was a much more serious issue! The article read,

Dalglish has succumbed to a troublesome ankle injury. Obviously this is a serious problem for the Liverpool manager, Bob Paisley, who has been fearing just such a breakdown. Dalglish has a fine record of survival against all of the tough tackling that comes his way and perhaps it will be helpful for Liverpool to see how his first absence in three years affects overall performance. Rush, bought from Chester for £300,000 last season, plays his first game. Mr Paisley said, 'It was not an easy decision, but what swayed me in the end was that if I had picked anyone else it would have meant playing them out of position. I have replaced a striker with a striker.'

So Rushie made his debut – but only because Bob didn't want to play another man out of position! From such inauspicious beginnings was a legend born, although Ian was initially peeved at his lack of opportunities and even considered leaving the club. Paisley told him his time would come and that he should be more selfish in front of goal. He eventually opened his scoring account after nine games and became a regular in the side – as Kenny's partner, rather than his replacement – in the 1981–82 season.

His first goal came on 30 September 1981, in the European Cup first-round, second-leg tie at Anfield against Oulun Palloseura. Liverpool had already won the first leg away in Finland 1–0 and now they crushed their opponents 7–0, Rushie netting on sixty-seven minutes after coming on as a sub for David Johnson. He scored his first league goal on 10 October 1981, in the 3–0 win over Leeds at Anfield, and a month later scored an even more important one in the 3–1 home demolition of neighbours Everton.

The boy was on his way to becoming a man and to becoming a goal-scoring Kop idol.

He ended the season as the club's top scorer, with thirty goals in forty-nine matches, seventeen of which came in the League as Liverpool won back the crown that Aston Villa had pinched in the previous campaign.

Rushie was also on target in the 1982 League Cup Final, grabbing Liverpool's third as they beat Spurs 3–1 at Wembley.

But his finest season would be the 1983–84 campaign, when he hit forty-seven goals, helping Liverpool to a remarkable array of trophies – the League title, European Cup and League

Cup. He won both the PFA and sportswriters' Player of the Year awards and his goal haul earned him the coveted Golden Boot, awarded to Europe's top goal-scorer each season.

That European Cup final win was all the more remarkable as Liverpool had to beat Roma in their home stadium (the Olympic stadium) – and in a tense penalty shootout. Rushie scored the fourth penalty as Liverpool went on to win 4–2 on penalties (after the match itself had ended 1–1) and lift their fourth European Cup in eight years. Liverpool's team was much changed from the one that had beaten Real Madrid to win the trophy three years previously. Ray Clemence, Phil Thompson, Terry McDermott and Ray Kennedy had gone, being replaced by Bruce Grobbelaar, Mark Lawrenson, Craig Johnston and, of course, Rushie. The team read: Grobbelaar, Neal, Lawrenson, Hansen, A. Kennedy, Lee, Johnston, Whelan, Souness, Rush, Dalglish.

Rushie would tell the excellent website, lfchistory.net, that, yes, the 1983 –84 season was his favourite in terms of goal-scoring achievement but that his favourite as a team player came two years later: 'Goal-scoring, yes [1983–84 was his favourite], but overall the season I enjoyed the most was 1985–86 when we won the double. As an individual it was maybe the 1983–84 season when I scored 47 goals but as a team it was when we won the double. To actually play in the first Merseyside cup final, against Everton. To be losing 1–0 at half-time and win 3–1 and score two goals. We had won the double. Everything rolled into one in this game, against the Everton team which was the second best team in Europe then.'

He would also tell the same site of his seemingly telepathic understanding with Dalglish: 'We didn't speak a lot off the pitch but on the pitch we just had a thing that was natural. I knew what Kenny was good at and Kenny knew what I was good at. That was what made us work so well as a pair. Kenny wouldn't look up to see where I was, he would just put the ball into space and I just knew Kenny was going to put the ball there. The defenders were just left thinking, "How does he know the ball was going to get there?" But we did know.'

Kenneth Mathieson Dalglish had arrived at Liverpool in 1977 with Bob Paisley, the club having had to fork out a British transfer record of £440,000 to secure his services from Celtic in Glasgow. Of course, it turned out to be money well spent; a bargain if you looked at the service and honours Kenny brought. He was already a major star in Scotland when he arrived as Keegan's replacement – with Celtic he had won four Scottish First Division titles, four Scottish Cups and one Scottish League Cup from 1971.

At Anfield he would comfortably surpass that haul, winning seven league titles, three European Cups and five domestic cups. As with Toshack and Rushie, the Liverpool fans initially had their reservations about the man who would become known to them as 'King Kenny'. Hardly surprising considering the act he had to follow: Keegan was the best player in England and Kenny had a major job on his hands to persuade the Anfield faithful he could take on his number-seven shirt and produce the same results.

But the man was a magician, a genius, the conductor of the orchestra, as Liverpool embarked on a period of domination in the domestic and European game.

Yes, he was as good as Keegan. Yes, he was better than Keegan – more naturally gifted and talented.

He scored his first goal for the club on his league debut against Middlesbrough on 20 August 1977. Three days later he also hit the net on his first appearance before the Anfield fans, who would come to adore him in the 2–0 victory over Newcastle.

At the end of his first season, Dalglish had hit a total of thirty-one goals in sixty-two matches. The final one was the most important – it won the European Cup for the club as they beat Bruges 1–0 at Wembley.

Two years later Rushie arrived at Anfield and the eighteen-year-old would eventually link up with Dalglish, by then twenty-nine, to form their wonderful partnership. The old head, with the ultimate footballing brain and the pace and goal-grabbing instincts of the young whippersnapper, combined to form a link-up that was irresistible and unstoppable. Kenny would score 172 goals in 515 games for Liverpool and would earn the accolade of being the club's best player ever from fans, players and managers for the outstanding thirteen years he graced Liverpool FC as a performer on the pitch.

In 1999 Alan Shearer and Michael Owen – no slouches in front of goal themselves – were asked by *Match of the Day* magazine to name the best strike force ever in British football. Inevitably, they plumped for the Ian Rush/Kenny Dalglish combo. Owen selected two of his Anfield predecessors as Shearer reflected on the skills of his former Newcastle manager: 'Rush was a class striker; deadly around the box and with a scoring instinct,' Owen said. Shearer purred when he spoke about King Kenny: 'He would take the defender out of the game with a pass and put backspin on the ball so it sat up, inviting the shot. Class.' Peter Beardsley and Gary Lineker – who scored thirty-six goals together as an England partnership – were voted runners-up, while Kevin Keegan and John Toshack were third.

The Rush/Dalglish partnership was an ominous target for Luis Suarez and Daniel Sturridge but both were as confident as their illustrious predecessors and both were natural goal-scorers. They might not have matched Ian and Kenny but I reckon Suarez, with his genius and goals, proved to be Liverpool's best individual buy since Kenny signed, back in the summer of 1977.

Luis Suarez was the new King of the Kop – and the fans just couldn't get enough of him. But now let's turn our attentions to the final stages of the 2013-14 season, as Luis and Daniel continued to combine to take Liverpool back into the promised land of the Champions League.

CHAPTER FIFTEEN

THE GREATEST

Steven Gerrard had publicly voiced his belief that Liverpool could win that first top-flight title since 1990 after he led the team to a stirring 3–0 win over Manchester United in March 2014. In the event, they would fall short but only by a wafer-thin margin – two points – as Manchester City's experience and strength in squad depth ultimately proved decisive. But to finish runners-up after their seventh-place finish the previous season, and with a squad that was clearly not as powerful all-round as City's and Chelsea's, was some superb achievement.

It meant that boss Brendan Rodgers had kept his promise to take Luis and Co. into the following season's Champions League and that Suarez would surely have no reason to leave Anfield now – even if Real Madrid continued to test the water in that typically underhand way they always do when they want to buy a quality player who is under contract. They let it slip that they were interested in Suarez through their media mouthpiece, the sports daily *Marca*, and the possibilities of a move snowballed from there, eventually reaching the English papers, who said Luis was 'likely to be a £70 million target for Real' in the summer of 2014.

But why would Luis want to leave Anfield? OK, Madrid are probably the most glamorous club in the world and they also have the most expensive players in the world but Luis was happy at Liverpool, with his family and was now going to show off his skills in the Champions League. Also, he still wanted to lift the Premier League trophy – not only for himself but for Steven Gerrard, whom he admitted was the best player he had ever worked with and a man he felt a great loyalty towards. Suarez knew what winning the league would mean to Stevie G and he was determined to bring the trophy to Anfield.

In the previous twelve months, he had also been accepted as a genius by the stars of the British game and the sports writers. He had won both the Professional Footballers' Player of the Year (PFA) and the Football Writers' Player of the Year awards. It was a remarkable turnaround for a player who had been widely condemned twelve months earlier after the 'bite incident' involving Branislav Ivanovic. Luis had come a mighty long way; he had avoided controversy on the pitch and had been lauded and rewarded with universal praise for his skills and goals. Of course, an unexpected event or setback – like biting an Italian in the 2014 World Cup – could wreck all his good work, make all the accolades seem redundant and have him heading out of the door to Spain, but to Barcelona instead of Madrid

The love and attachment he felt for Liverpool FC was clear for all to see when he hid his face under his shirt after the 3–3 draw at Crystal Palace in May 2014. Of course, Liverpool had led 3–0 only to throw two points away by allowing Palace to come back into the game late on. Luis was hugged by Gerrard as the result sank in... along with the inevitable feeling that their title challenge was now effectively over. I am told that Luis 'was devastated'; that he realised it was now 'very unlikely' that Manchester City would mess up with two home games. Luis knew that victory in those two matches would see City lifting the Premier League title, whatever Liverpool did in their remaining game against Newcastle at Anfield. And he was proved right as City overcame their own nerves to overwhelm Aston Villa and West Ham to finish champions. It was a crushing blow for Suarez and Gerrard but it meant the likelihood of Luis now leaving for Madrid had become still more remote, as he still desperately wanted to win the league with Liverpool.

After their 3–0 win at United in March, Liverpool won their next six league games to challenge for the title. Earlier in the campaign it had appeared that they would be happy to settle for fourth place in the league and one of the four Champions League places available. But as the team's form improved and they continued to lash home the goals, expectations changed dramatically. Winning those six matches on top of the triumph at Old Trafford had their fans believing that this could, indeed, be the season when they finally took the top-league crown back to Anfield.

They would fall short by those two points to City but it had still, undoubtedly, been a brilliant season for Suarez and his team-mates. They had exceeded all expectations and raised hopes that the next campaign could, indeed, be the one in which Liverpool won the title.

Directly after trouncing Man United, they went to Cardiff and the goals continued to flow as they returned home with a 6–3 win under their belts. The philosophy of the football team mirrored that of the legendary Brazilian national sides; that invariably shipped goals but always believed they had the strikers to steer them to victory. It was a case of 'we'll outscore you' and Liverpool, under Rodgers, seemed to have bought into that entertaining philosophy. It meant watching Liverpool was never dull: no, it was wonderful, with goals and thrills and spills galore. In this endearing kingdom of end-to-end football, Luis Suarez ruled. He was the man who outscored everyone and the man whose passion and commitment spurred his team on to the highest of heights.

He may not have been the skipper but he was the leader of the gang. His team-mates knew they could rely on him to hit the back of the net, whatever the situation and whoever they were playing. In the victory at Cardiff, Luis grabbed a hat-trick to equal Robbie Fowler's twenty-eight-goal record for a Liverpool Premier League season – and there were still eight league games to go. It was little wonder that Luis was already being hailed as Liverpool's greatest striker EVER.

Luis walked away with the match ball as a reward for his hat-trick and the chants of his adoring fans ringing in his ears. Then his manager joined in the praise, saying, 'Luis's determination, his desire, his will is at such a big level. He is a world-class player who is enjoying his football, and long may it continue. The mental resilience is how we've grown over the past eighteen months, and that confidence to know we can get back in the game. You look at our imagination and creativity today. I think the crowd felt that every time we were in their half, we could score. We've got footballers, technicians, who can open up a game for us.' That was a nice way to put it: Suarez was a football technician; a genius who had the skills to destroy any opposition.

Even Brendan Rodgers' Cardiff counterpart was fulsome in his analysis of Suarez. Ole Gunnar Solskjaer added, 'Luis Suarez is a top, top striker. He is always on the move and is so difficult to mark.'

Four days after the win at Cardiff, Liverpool had the chance to record a victory over another set of relegation strugglers. Sunderland arrived at Anfield needing a point or three to lift their morale but ended up going back to the north-east with nothing as their hosts won 2–1. For once, Suarez was not on the score sheet, as goals from Gerrard and Sturridge left the Black Cats still three points away from safety. But Sturridge's goal meant that, for the first time in fifty years, two Liverpool strikers (himself and Luis) had scored twenty league goals in a season – and, of course, there were plenty more to come. The win was Liverpool's seventh in a row and meant they maintained their battle to win the league, in second place, just a point behind leaders Chelsea.

Manchester City were two points behind Liverpool but had two games in hand and were still the favourites to win the title. They had the best squad in the league, with players costing £20 million and upwards regularly warming the bench. Chelsea enjoyed similar riches and it was to Brendan Rodgers's credit that he was masterminding a title charge with much more limited resources. Yet he was fortunate in that he had Suarez – undoubtedly the best striker in British football and, arguably, the best on the planet.

The pressure was increasing every week as it now became apparent that Liverpool were, indeed, genuine title contenders, rather than a team whose ambition was simply to make it into the top four. The goal posts for Suarez and Co. had certainly moved since the start of the season when the club's fans admitted they would be delighted with a top-four finish. Now, with appetites whetted by the team's wonderful unbeaten run, dreams of lifting the title itself were being articulated. It was a reflection of the brilliant job Rodgers had done but the boss didn't want his men to be tripped up by nerves so he cleverly kept the pressure on rivals City, publicly maintaining they were the favourites and that anything beyond a top-four finish would be a wonderful added bonus for Liverpool.

Rodgers said, 'It's up to other teams to lose, so we will keep working hard. If City win their games, they win. It's simple maths. I'm concentrating on my team and Jose Mourinho is saying what I'm saying. Manchester City have games in hand and the squad to win the title and the Champions League, Chelsea likewise, but we are enjoying being up there.'

Rodgers did, however, lavish praise on Suarez and Sturridge for their achievement of twenty goals apiece in the league.

He said, 'It is a great achievement for the team. Suarez and Sturridge are soloists, individuals that fit into the collective picture. They are top-class talents.'

By the end of March, the games were continuing to come fast and furious. No sooner had Liverpool defeated Sunderland than Tottenham were arriving at Anfield under the watchful eye of caretaker head coach Tim Sherwood. Sherwood was desperate for a good result at Anfield to prove he had the credentials to do the job on a permanent basis but he would head back to London 'gutted and angry' after Suarez inspired Liverpool to a crushing 4–0 victory. Luis grabbed the second of the four goals and the result meant that Liverpool were top of the league. The Uruguayan also had a header deflected onto the post as his speed and agility proved too much for a leaden-footed Tottenham backline.

This was why Luis had joined Liverpool in the first place: to help propel them back to the top of the English Premier League. He knew all about the club's fantastic history, its wonderfully loyal fans and how much it meant to them to return to the pinnacle. He had always believed he could score the goals that would bring the title back to Anfield after so many years and now they were top. 'From that win over Tottenham to the very end of the season, Luis was like a man on a mission,' I was told by a source. 'Winning the title meant everything to him. Liverpool had been top on Boxing Day and he had been low when they were knocked off the summit. So after the win over Spurs, he was determined to do all he could to ensure they ended top at the end of the season. He had taken Ajax back to the very top and he fully intended to do the same with

Liverpool. He is a man who sets his sights on something and does everything in his power to achieve it.'

Admirable as that was, the stark truth was that, although third-placed Manchester City were four points behind, they had two games in hand. And Chelsea, who were second, were just a point behind. Wins over the likes of Tottenham were essential but the key matches would be the home games against City and Chelsea, which loomed large the following month.

'Luis knew those two matches would hold the key to the season and whether he would be lifting the league title,' my source added, 'and he couldn't wait to take on City and Chelsea. He always wanted to play the best to show that he was the best.'

Boss Rodgers also accepted that the two games lurking on the horizon would give a true indication of how far his team had come and whether they could lift the title, or how far away they remained from doing so. After the Spurs win, he said,

We all want to win the title. It has been a long time. We just need to prepare and do well and, if we do that, we will win games.

Chelsea and Manchester City understand Anfield will be a real tough place to come. We love playing here, the support was incredible and that will only intensify. We respect Chelsea – they have a world-class manager and a team that has been assembled to win the Champions League and the Premier League. Manchester City are one of the new super-powers in world football but we feel we can win any game because we are a team, we have a lot of hunger and our tactical ideas are improving all the time.

However, Rodgers said it was highly unlikely that his team could win the league as they did not have the depth of quality in their overall squad. He said he wasn't indulging in mind games and that he never played them. That struck me as true. He was an honest man and always up front and transparent in his press conferences at Liverpool. This was a man you could believe in and take at face value for his comments and beliefs. However, the same could not be said of Chelsea boss Jose Mourinho, who similarly claimed his team could not win the league because they were like 'a little horse' compared with Manuel Pellegrini's thoroughbreds at City. Mourinho was a master of the dark arts and would use any ploy to niggle his rivals. He claimed City were nailed-on winners of the league because of their squad strength but most hacks in the Premier League press boxes up and down the country believed he WAS indulging in mind games. That he was trying his damnedest to crank up the pressure on Pellegrini and City.

One thing Rodgers knew for sure was that his Liverpool would need to continue their unbeaten run if they were to lift the title. They would need to beat City and Chelsea during April 2014, when both teams were scheduled to play at Anfield. But before that there was the small matter of a tough-looking away fixture at Upton Park. Rodgers' men proved how committed they were to keeping up their title-winning potential by securing a 2–1 victory in east London.

Suarez failed to add to his tally of twenty-nine goals for the season but two Steven Gerrard penalty conversions earned the three points. I am told Luis was simply happy that the run towards the title had continued. He loved scoring goals but he was also a firm believer in the team ethic. He knew that his goals by themselves would not be enough to win the league; that it would take a concerted team effort from defence to attack. So he left the Boleyn Ground contented as the team coach pulled away from east London and headed back to Liverpool. It had been a case of mission accomplished: the team would still be top of the league when Man City arrived the following Sunday in what would definitely be a key clash and one more step towards the title if he and his Liverpool team-mates could see off the challenge of City, whom Rodgers declared were their main challengers.

He said, 'City will be looking to get a result next Sunday. For us, we are just going to enjoy it. We know it's a big game. But in the big games this season, we've tended to do well. The mentality here is to be fearless. We will respect the opposition but it's about ourselves.'

Liverpool had lost 2–1 in the reverse fixture at the Etihad the previous Boxing Day but had done enough to win the match. Speaking on the BBC's *Match of the Day* programme, City skipper Vincent Kompany admitted that his team had had to battle to win that match and said that Liverpool were the best team they had come up against. Kompany said, 'They are the strongest team we have played this season. They have a great squad and they are not there by luck. We have different styles but the same philosophy of trying to score goals, so I think it will be an entertaining game.'

Well, Kompany certainly wasn't wrong on that score. The match would end in a 3–2 victory for Liverpool over City and brought back memories of the Liverpool-Newcastle game at Anfield at the same stage of the season in 1996. It ended 4–3 to the hosts and was one of the finest adverts ever for the quality, passion and entertainment of the Premier League. The match in 2014 against City also had everything: supreme thrills and spills, goals galore and all delivered within the framework of attacking, entertaining football from both teams. Liverpool raced into a 2–0 lead, only for City to peg them back at 2–1 and, as it seemed City would go on to win, up popped Brazilian ace Coutinho to send the Kop into rhapsody. It proved to be another blank day for Suarez, as he failed to get onto the scoresheet and earned a booking for a foul on Martin Demichelis.

Luis was actually lucky that he wasn't sent off for a second yellow-card offence when he made a meal of a challenge by Demichelis. He hit the ground as if he had been shot, but ref Mark Clattenburg let him off the hook. One of the strongest images was of Steven Gerrard addressing his men in a huddle at the end of the game, imploring them to not slacken off now and to go to relegation strugglers Norwich with the same attitude they had shown to overcome City. Gerrard told the players, 'This does not fucking slip now. Listen. Listen. This is gone. We go to Norwich. Exactly the same. We go again. Come on!'

After the match Brendan Rodgers said, 'The message is just

to continue. We don't need to change. We play with no fear, whether it's a big opponent like Manchester City or Norwich next week.' Luis was as revved up as the rest of his team-mates as he listened to an emotional Gerrard in the huddle in the middle of the pitch, nodding his head in agreement at his skipper and clenching his fist in determination as he left the pitch. He knew what winning the league would mean to the club and he was desperate to lift the trophy for Gerrard, whom he admitted was probably the best player he had ever had as a team-mate. The bond between the two ran deep and their mutual admiration and respect was clear to see.

And the skipper's rallying call made much sense. It would have been easy enough for some players to think they had done the hard bit by beating Man City and that Norwich would be a walkover. But Gerrard knew that the hard bit was actually avoiding any complacency whatsoever as they approached the match at Carrow Road. Norwich were scrapping for their Premier League lives and presented as much danger as City. 'Luis backed Steven to the hilt in his analysis of the Norwich away game,' I was told. 'He realised the dangers of going there and thinking it was going to be a walk in the park. Luis and Steven were carved from the same mettle; they were two warriors who walked side by side with one common aim – to make Liverpool the best team in England.'

It was lucky that the dynamic duo did gee up their troops and led by determined example, as Norwich most certainly were not a walkover on the day. Liverpool had to scrap all the way to wrap up another valuable three points as their hosts battled passionately in front of their fans. Of course, it was little wonder that Luis enjoyed playing against Norwich. He had a dazzling record of scoring against them in recent seasons, including four goals the previous December when he spearheaded Liverpool's 5–1 league triumph over the Canaries at Anfield. He had failed to find the back of the net in the Reds' previous two games – against West Ham and Man City – but, inevitably, was back in business at Carrow Road as Liverpool ran out 3–2 winners. Luis's strike was sandwiched between a Raheem Sterling brace as Liverpool showed they could grind out results when needed. The win lifted them five points clear of the pack at the top of the league after second-placed Chelsea recorded a shock 2–1 home loss to another team of relegation stragglers, Sunderland.

For Luis, his goal marked yet another stat for the history books in his incredible career. It was his thirtieth league goal of the season and meant he had become the first Liverpool player since Ian Rush in 1986–87 to reach that remarkable milestone. After the match, Luis admitted he was 'very proud' to have equalled Rush's record but said it was more important that the team won and maintained their position at the top. He said, 'It was an important win for us. We worked very hard today. It was important we stayed calm. I'm proud of my thirty goals but it's more important for the team to win.'

The win at Norwich also meant Liverpool had sealed qualification for the group stages of the Champions League, thus achieving the ambition set down by Brendan Rodgers at the beginning of the campaign with three games to go. The Liverpool manager was delighted, saying, 'I want to say a massive congratulations to the players because our objective at the beginning of the season was to qualify for the Champions League. That was always going to be an incredibly tough task because of the competition there is at this level but we know after this victory that we can't finish any lower than third, so that puts us into the group stages.

'It's great for the supporters and we now go into the last three games looking to perform well and continue with the wins.'

And Suarez and Co. didn't need it spelling out that a win in their next match would put them within touching distance of the title. Yes, Jose Mourinho was due in town with his Chelsea team, who were battling Liverpool and City for the crown. It was a case of 'one down, one to go' – Liverpool had beaten City in an exhilarating game of football that had shown just why the English Premier League was rated the best in the world: attacking, entertaining football, goals and incidents galore and two teams playing to win on the front foot.

But Mourinho would pose a very different problem. He had returned to Chelsea for a second time the previous summer after spells in Italy (with Inter Milan) and Spain (Real Madrid). On his arrival back at Stamford Bridge he had declared himself 'The Happy One' and spoke of how he was going to forge an attack-minded team for owner Roman Abramovich. But that ideal didn't last long. As soon as Chelsea started leaking goals, Mourinho went back to basics, making the Blues hard to beat and an outfit that would strike on the counter attack. This had been his way, how he set up his teams throughout his career and he now arrived at Anfield determined to smother Liverpool's wonderful, attacking football with his game-killing tactics. He had seen how Man City had lost trying to take the hosts on at their own game and was determined that his team would definitely not suffer a similar fate. Mourinho arrived at Anfield with the sole intention of putting a spoke in Liverpool's title hopes – and he left having done just that, as Chelsea won 2–0.

The result meant that Chelsea were now two points behind Liverpool and, more ominously, Man City had moved to within three points, with a game in hand and a better goal difference. Mourinho had blown a hole in Liverpool's title hopes by 'parking two buses' according to a despondent and rightly critical Brendan Rodgers. The Liverpool boss had served under Mourinho during his first spell at Stamford Bridge but the protégé was now openly critical of his one-time mentor. Of course, Rodgers was upset that his team had lost their impetus in the title battle but he also made the valid point that Chelsea had won with an anti-football manifesto.

Goals from Demba Ba, at the end of the first half, and Willian, at the end of the ninety minutes, undid Liverpool. The opener was, of course, ironic, in that skipper Gerrard slipped on the turf to allow Ba through on goal. After the match against City, he had urged his players in a huddle not to let it slip in the following match at Norwich. Now he had slipped up himself – but no Liverpool fan would criticise him. On numerous occasions throughout the season it had been Gerrard's determination and drive that had seen Liverpool home. It was simply unfortunate and a cruel twist of fate that it had been the skipper who suffered the mishap.

Afterwards Rodgers said,

They parked two buses, rather than one. From the first minute they had ten men behind the ball. We are a team that tried to win the game, in a sporting manner. We were the team trying to win but we just couldn't make the breakthrough. We were the better team with the ball. We just could not unlock them. It was difficult because they virtually played right from the off with a back six. They had a back four, with two wingers back and then the midfield three in front of them. Just putting ten players right on your eighteen-yard box is not difficult to coach but it is obviously much harder to try and break through it.

Gerrard was distraught and so was Suarez. He didn't need telling that the initiative was now with Man City. Put simply, if they won their remaining league games, they would pip Liverpool to the league title… whatever Liverpool did. The pressure was on and it was imperative that Liverpool now won their next match at Crystal Palace if they were to keep turning the screw on City. But after leading 3–0 with eleven minutes to go, they ended up drawing 3–3. Suarez had grabbed the third goal for Liverpool, firing home for his thirty-first league goal of the campaign. But he was in tears at the end with the realisation that the dream was as good as over. The point had taken Liverpool back to the top but City now needed only to win their remaining two games – both at home – and the title would end up in Manchester. And as the games were against two teams who had little to battle for – Aston Villa and West Ham – Luis believed the game was up.

He had to be helped off the field at Selhurst Park, his shirt covering his face, his skipper leading him down the tunnel with a consoling hug. It was one of the saddest moments of Suarez's career; he had been so determined to lift that league title with Liverpool. Now City would win their remaining matches, which meant that Liverpool's 2–1 home win over Newcastle in their remaining game could not affect the outcome.

But Suarez and his team-mates had defied all expectations in finishing runners-up and notching more than a hundred league goals for only the second time in their history. It was some achievement, given that in the previous season they had finished SEVENTH and it provided genuine optimism that, given some key summer signings, Liverpool would soon go one better and bring that elusive title back to Anfield.

Of course, it would be essential that Luis Suarez stay with the club for that dream to be realised. He had proved himself a world-class striker and no amount of money, or replacements, would be able to compensate if he was allowed to leave. 'It could be like Tottenham, after they let Gareth Bale go to Madrid,' I was told by lifelong Liverpool fan Roy Stone. 'Spurs got £86 million and spent it on new players but they weren't half as good as when they had Bale. Letting Luis go could have the same outcome: it is vital that the club keep him if they want to go on and win the league.'

I was also told that Suarez was 'gutted' at Liverpool's last-gasp blow-up in the title race but that he 'felt part of it all' at the club and wanted to stay for at least one more season to help 'bring the title home where it belonged'. The 2013–14 campaign had certainly belonged to Luis: he had propelled

Liverpool to that runners-up spot with his goals and had won awards galore personally. There was the PFA Players' Player of the Year and the Football Writers' Player of the Year gongs and, as the season ended, he also received the Barclays Player of the Season award and the Barclays Golden Boot award for those thirty-one league goals in thirty-three appearances.

Many fans were now of the opinion that Luis Suarez wasn't simply the best Liverpool player of the current era but that he could be mentioned in such coveted company as Kenny Dalglish and Ian Rush as Liverpool's number-one player of all time. As Jamie Carragher put it, 'I think, in terms of ability as a player, he could be the best player to play for Liverpool.' And, as Steven Gerrard added, 'I have played with some top players over the years at this club – world-class players – but for me, Luis is in a league of his own.'

Praise indeed, and well warranted too. The era of Luis Suarez, the greatest, was upon us – and Liverpool's loyal army of fans just couldn't get enough of their hero as they dreamed of winning the league title and then the Champions League. With his world-class talent and goals, he was the man they trusted to lead them back to the promised land.

But nothing was ever straightforward with Luis – and, yes, there would be a final twist in our tale as he headed for the 2014 World Cup in Brazil. And it was a twist in the tale that would leave every Liverpool fan feeling gutted.

EPILOGUE

There's a saying in life that the true definition of insanity is doing the same thing time after time and expecting a different outcome. Even hardened football hacks like myself can get caught out with it sometimes. I had completed the previous chapter about Luis and how he had matured at Liverpool under Brendan Rodgers, and how he richly deserved his double Player of the Year awards, only for the brilliant but unpredictable striker to then go and turn it all upside down by biting Italy's Giorgio Chiellini at the 2014 World Cup in Brazil.

After all that Luis had achieved in his remarkable 2013-14 season at Anfield, it was a real out-of-the-blue kick in the guts; a letdown and a true low. Luis had hit the self-destruct button in the worst way possible as that old red mist descended upon him and he reverted to type with the chomp on Chiellini's shoulder. It proved the old saying about insanity had some substance – after all, this was the third time Suarez had bitten an opponent following those attacks on Otman Bakkal when he was with Ajax in Amsterdam and Branislav Ivanovic with Liverpool.

And the outcome would be similar to those earlier incidents as he now faced disciplinary measures – but the severity of the punishment would change. Precisely because it was the third bite of his career, he would receive a much more severe censure, as football's world governing body Fifa came down hard on him with a four-month worldwide football ban. He was also ruled out of nine international matches and sent home immediately from the World Cup in disgrace. If he stayed at Liverpool – and it was now widely accepted that he would quit for Barcelona – he would miss the first nine matches of the 2014-15 season.

Was the punishment too severe? I believe it was, in the sense that it was purely censure without any attempt to help the player resolve his mental problems. He obviously had demons that he could not control – demons that could probably be traced back to his father deserting him at an early age and his need to duck and dive to survive in Montevideo as a very troubled youngster. This was not someone who had become the best striker in the world with a settled, middle-class upbringing like, for example, Brazil's Kaka. No, this was a boy who had had to fight for everything; nothing had come to him on a plate. So it might have been more constructive, not to say compassionate, for Fifa to have also offered an element of help to him along with their wrath. They could have directed him into a programme of rehabilitation – with anger management and CBT therapy – rather than simply punishing him heavily with no thoughts of helping him conquer the very demons that had led him to bite a player again.

No one is arguing that he did not need to be punished, but Fifa arguably appeared to be keen to prove they were no soft touch – that they could, and would, come down hard on offenders if need be. Yet this was the very same organisation that regularly turned a blind eye to racism with soft financial fines for countries where it was rife at international football matches, and an organisation that was regularly accused of being corrupt and immoral. Given the bad press it had only recently received over the handing of the 2022 World Cup to Qatar, was it possible that the Suarez punishment was simply an attempt to deflect criticism and to prove that it was a credible, reputable organisation? If so, the stench of corruption and mismanagement over the Qatar debacle would still not go away even with the Suarez issue dominating the sports news agenda.

Initially, Luis denied he had bitten Chiellini, telling Fifa's disciplinary panel that he did not deliberately sink his teeth into the player, and that he was the person who was left in the most pain. 'In no way it happened how you have described, as a bite or intent to bite,' he said in a letter to the panel. 'After the impact... I lost my balance, making my body unstable and falling on top of my opponent. At that moment I hit my face against the player leaving a small bruise on my cheek and a strong pain in my teeth.'

Fifa dismissed the claim and hit Luis hard, with the

suggestion from sources close to the world football body suggesting the player's punishment was so harsh because he had not admitted the offence or shown any remorse for his actions.

Eventually, Luis would apologise to Chiellini, in a statement on his Twitter account, as he appealed against the four-month ban. Luis said, 'After several days being home with my family I have had the opportunity to regain my calm and reflect on the reality of what occurred during the Italy-Uruguay match. Independent from the fallout and contradicting declarations that have surfaced during these past few days, all of which have been without the intention of interfering with the good performance of my national team, the truth is my colleague Giorgio Chiellini suffered the physical result of a bite in the collision he suffered with me.

'For this I deeply regret what occurred, apologise to Giorgio Chiellini and the entire football family and I vow to the public there will never be another incident like it.'

Chiellini responded swiftly on his own Twitter account, accepting the apology. 'It's all forgotten,' he wrote. 'I hope Fifa will reduce your suspension.'

It was suggested that Luis had only apologised after pressure from Barcelona FC, who remained keen on signing him but did not want their own good name tarnished. The fact that Luis did not mention Liverpool FC, or apologise to them, added weight to the speculation. If Luis did join Barca, it would be a dream move for him. He had always wanted to play for them and his in-laws lived in the Catalan city.

But I was told he also loved Liverpool the city, Liverpool the football club and that he felt a close allegiance to the Liverpool fans who had stood by him during his various misdemeanors, so it was far from a certainty that he would want to walk away from Anfield.

The unfortunate truth for Liverpool FC was this: despite all the baggage he carried, they still needed Luis Suarez far more than he needed them. Without his goals and passionate contribution during the 2013-14 campaign, they would not have qualified for the Champions League. It was a sobering thought to wrestle with for Brendan Rodgers and his staff – and the loyal fans – as Luis's future remained up in the air.

His departure would bring in a huge transfer fee, but would Liverpool be able to still compete at the very top without him? Even with the arrival of expensive players to replace him?

As far as the World Cup of 2014 was concerned, Luis's disgrace was a personal disaster for him and a terrible blow for Uruguay. He had shown exactly why any team would be willing to pay upwards of £80million for him as he destroyed England with two wonder goals in the group stage – when he was only 75 per cent fit. England's vulnerable backline simply could not handle his speed and cunning as he sent them packing just weeks after an operation on his left knee.

He had picked up the injury while training for the World Cup and an MRI scan on 21 May found damage to the meniscus. Luis had keyhole surgery and his recovery confounded the football world. Against England he was unstoppable, and he then went on to help his country beat the Italians in the final group game and to qualify for the last 16 clash with Colombia.

But the bite on Chiellini ended his participation in the

tournament – and effectively ended his country's too. Without their talisman, Uruguay crashed out 2-0 as the Colombians, spearheaded by the genius of James Rodriguez, confirmed their position as dark horses for the world crown.

Who knows what the result would have been with Suarez in action? It would surely have been a much closer game. Luis's actions had cost him and his country dear: he could have gone down in the history books as the greatest player at the 2014 World Cup. The man who lifted a nation to its greatest triumph: a modern-day Maradona who almost single-handedly led his country to an unlikely World Cup triumph.

Unfortunately, he will, like Maradona in 1994, now be remembered for all the wrong reasons. Just as Diego was kicked out of the tournament in America that year for drug abuse, so the name of Suarez will now always be tarnished by his own shameful exit for biting an opponent in Brazil. And that is perhaps the saddest consequence for Luis Suarez after his moment of madness in June 2014.